INTOXERATED

INTOXERATED

THE DEFINITIVE DRINKER'S DICTIONARY

PAUL DICKSON

ILLUSTRATED BY BRIAN REA

MELVILLE HOUSE
BROOKLYN · LONDON

© 2009, 2012 Paul Dickson
Illustrations © 2009 Brian Rea

Previously published as *Drunk* in 2009

Melville House Publishing
145 Plymouth Street
Brooklyn, NY 11201

www.mhpbooks.com

ISBN: 978-1-61219-143-0

First Melville House Printing: September 2012

Book design: Kelly Blair

Manufactured in the United States of America
1 2 3 4 5 6 7 8 9 10

The Library of Congress cataloged the original hardcover edition as follows:

Dickson, Paul.
 Drunk : the definitve drinker's dictionary / by Paul Dickson.
   p. cm.
 Includes bibliographical references.
 ISBN 978-1-933633-75-6
 1. Drinking of alcoholic beverages--Dictionaries. 2. Drinking of alcoholic
beverages--Quotations, maxims, etc. 3. Drinking of alcoholic beverages--
Miscellanea. 4. Drinking of alcoholic beverages in literature. I. Title.
 PN56.D8D53 2009
 394.1'303--dc22

                         2009028423

GETTING TO 3,000

In the brief time since the first edition of this book a list of new synonyms have managed to be coined or re-discovered. Adding these to the earlier list brings the total to 2,985 synonyms for various states of intoxication, up from 2,964 in the last edition and a vast improvement from my original 1983 compilation of 2,231—which allowed me to become a record-holder in the Guinness Book of World Records for the most synonyms for a single word. I believe we can reach my ultimate goal of 3,000 in the not too distant future. Once this is attained, I will be able to turn my full attention to the Annotated Registry of Ice Cream Flavors.

—Paul Dickson

Here are the latest additions to the *Intoxerated* list:

Baloobas

Bartuned: As if one's head is lying on the bar to hear it better.

Buffing the floor: As in, "He was buffing the floor." Overheard at a Brooklyn, NY art opening.

Creamolated: As in, "He was totally creamolated."

Doing an/the elephant: "When you sit at the end of the bar

and get so inebriated that you fall forward onto the bar, with one hand hanging over the edge like an elephant trunk."
(Heard in Bar 68, Dumbo, Brooklyn, New York)

Flapjacked: From Tom Wolfe's novel *I Am Charlotte Simmons*.

In the horrors

Intoxerated: A coinage blending intoxicated + inebriated. It is the sole term created by the compiler and is used for the title of this edition of the list.

Making Virginia fences: Discussing rural Virginia land-scapes during the era of Thomas Jefferson, Alan Pell Crawford observed in *Twilight at Monticello: The Final Years of Thomas Jefferson*, "The fences that enclosed these farmlands and kept livestock from wandering off were constructed in a zigzag arrangement so haphazard that New Englanders made a joke of it: when a man was drunk, they would say he was 'making Virginia fences.'"

Mellowed as casks

Moroculous

Perved

Schwasted

Skinko

Slizzered

Smiling as the grass: Common Australian term—it appears, for example, in *The Adventures of Barry McKenzie* by Barry Humphries.

Stiffer than a new broom

Stiffer'n a goat with rigor mortis: From *The Patriot Game* by George V. Higgins, 1982.

Watering the tonsils: Found in Australian mystery writer Peter Temple's *Bad Debts*.

Well potted

Wroughted

INTRODUCTION

The English language includes more synonyms for "drunk" than for any other word. I suggest there are several reasons why this is so:

Firstly, the condition, which is self-imposed, invites words implying folly, foolishness and self-inflicted dementia. People who are drunk look funny—not necessarily ha-ha funny—but odd-looking. There is a slurring of speech and lack of visual focus that inspires wordplay.

Secondly, drinkers and those who fuel them feel more comfortable euphemizing their condition. Better to say that one was "a little squiffy" last night than to admit intoxication.

Thirdly, there is the potential for libel that comes with calling somebody drunk. This is especially true in the United Kingdom, where it is relatively easy to sue for libel and even the most salacious tabloid will use a softer term. "Tired and emotional" is the most famous such British euphemism. While in the US, journalists will describe someone as "outgoing" to imply a happy drunk and "ruddy-faced" as a pure drunk.

And finally, I believe, as the late Stuart Flexner proposed in *I Hear America Talking*, the reason there are so many words for drunk is that people get drunk for different reasons and it affects them in different ways. So the vast English lexicon of synonyms simply reflects these many feelings and reactions.

The first person to ever collect and publish a sampling from the cornucopia of English slang for drunkenness was Benjamin Franklin, who included 228 terms for intoxication in his *Drinker's Dictionary* in 1737. A close student of human nature, as well as a man devoted to honesty in speech, writing and character, Franklin published his list not only to ridicule drunkenness but to expose the lengths of euphemism people would resort to, rather than to say outright that a person was drunk

Others followed Franklin's lead in this quirky list-making pursuit. Tom Paine published a small list in a 1794 joke book/comic almanac, *Tom Paine's Jests*. Charles Dickens' own small list appeared in his *Household Words*. Ambrose Bierce published a collection of 25 new words and phrases in 1882. And the lexically adventurous H. L. Mencken added to Franklin's list in his *The American Language*, published in 1921—the early days of Prohibition. Mencken created quite a stir when he described himself as "omnibibulous" (meaning that he drank anything and everything alcoholic). "I drink exactly as much as I want, and one drink more," he boasted. Edmund Wilson, in his 1927 "The Lexicon of Prohibition," produced a list of 105 terms in ascending order of drunkenness: from mild intoxication, "lit," to total incapacitation, "blotto." And Langston Hughes, in his 1958 column "How Many Words for Drunk," in the *Chicago Defender*, created a list of his own.

The "drunk" list-making has continued down the years, with diligent lexicographers tracking and recording along the way our collective inventiveness. I myself have dreamt about setting the "drunk" list record. And back in 1983 I succeeded, with the kind help of many, in setting the *Guinness Book of World Records* record for the most synonyms for a word—with 2,231 words and phrases for drunkenness. It was a record that I held until 1993 when I convinced Mark Young, the American *Guinness* editor, that I had a new list which appeared in *The Dickson Word Treasury*, which came in at 2,660 entries supplanting my old *Guinness* record with a gain of 429 terms.

But a record is a demanding thing to maintain. The language keeps growing and changing. And that change has only been accelerating under the explosive influence of technology. List-making as a pursuit has mushroomed in the Internet era. I am especially interested in the impact of text messaging on the creation of new words, abbreviations and emoticons. So it seemed that the time was ripe for a new list that brings together the ancient and the up-to-date, Chaucer's English with iPhone English.

So, with the help of many fine lexicographers, researchers, doctors, bartenders, strangers and friends, I submit this, my latest list of 2,964 synonyms for soused, with just a few final caveats.

    1. All the words and phrases are in "as found" condition, which means that mostly all of the terms with a personal pronoun refer to men (e.g. Dipped his bill, Has his pots on, etc.). No slight to besotted women is intended.

2. With a few exceptions I have limited this list to terms in English. The exceptions are terms that have come into English by virtue of common use.

3. Included are three mountweazels. A *mountweazel* is a term for a bogus entry in a dictionary or encyclopedia as a means of entrapping copyright violators. It dates from the 1975 edition of the *New Columbia Encyclopedia* and its entry for Lillian Virginia Mountweazel, "a photographer born in Bangs, Ohio, in 1942 only to die at age 31 in an explosion while working on assignment for *Combustibles* magazine." This work contains three such entries, coined and defined by writer William C. Young.

4. In no way is this work intended as a celebration of a serious social illness which accounts for tremendous pain to many, but rather as a celebration of the English language and all its euphemistic splendor.

THE ANNOTATED LIST

●

[:*) and Other Emoticons]

:*) : This is the accepted text message for "drunk" and represents the keyboard image of a drunk smile. In her October 7, 2007, review of the *Dictionary of American Slang*, the fourth edition of Robert L. Chapman's classic, edited by Barbara Ann Kipfer, Jan Freeman wrote: "And here's a sign of the times: The list of synonyms for 'drunk' and 'high' is two pages shorter than the list of abbreviations used in cell phone text messaging."

%*} : Inebriated, as distinguished from:

%-} : Intoxicated

[0-9]

12 gauged
40 under
45 degrees listed
86'ed

[A]

A brewer: *also* Half-a-brewer
A couple of chapters into the novel
A cup too much: *also* Has a cup too much
➤ **A CUT LEG**
A full cargo aboard: *also* Has a full cargo
A guest in the attic: *also* Has a guest in the attic
A passenger in the Cape Ann stage: An example of an intensely local construction which was listed in "Drunk," a list in the *Weekly Eagle*, Brattleboro, Vermont, July 15, 1851, that favored curt descriptions of the condition "hot," "high," "cut," "sawed," etc. The phrase appears in many collections of drunk terms but without explanation.
A peg too low: *also* Pegged too low
A piece of bread and cheese in the head: *also* Has a piece of bread and teeth in the head
A public mess
A Weeble: *also* Weeble wobbled; Weebled: From the name of the toy Weeble: "Weebles wobble but they don't fall down."
A write-off
Aboard
About blowed his top
About done
About to cave in

A CUT LEG

About to chunder: Chunder = vomit; to vomit

Above par: "Tolerably drunk" according to the glossary appended to George MacDonald Fraser's *Black Ajax*.

Absent

Absolutely done

Accidentally horizontal: From a "Politically Correct Guide" circulating on the Internet: "He is not FALLING DOWN DRUNK—He becomes ACCIDENTALLY HORIZONTAL."

Aced

Across the line: *also* Over the line

Activated

Acts like a fool: Reminder that Benjamin Franklin said in *Poor Richard's Almanac*, "Nothing more like a Fool than a drunken Man."

Adam's apple up

Addled

Admiral of the narrow seas: "A drunk who throws up in someone's lap," according to *The Vulgar Tongue*, a slang dictionary originally published in 1785 and oft reprinted through the year 2000.

Adrian: *also* Adrian Quist: Eponymous Australian rhyming slang for "pissed." Adrian Quist (1913-1991) was a Hall of Fame tennis player who was three-time Australian Championships men's singles champion. Dr. Antonio Lillo reports: "The term has been used since the 1970s. It is sometimes shortened to 'Adrian.'" (as above)

Advanced intoxication: Often used by police to describe someone who is dead drunk.

Afflicted

Afloat

Ah-wat-si: Blackfoot term which means "crazy-brave," cited in *Forest and Stream* magazine, July 18, 1903.

Airlocked

Alcoholed up

Alcoholic

Alcoholic sprightliness

Alcoholic synonymous: Noted on a tee-shirt during the summer of 2008.

Alcoholized

Alcoholled

Alecie: *also* Alecied: Pronounced ale-see

Aled up

Ale-washed

Alight

Alkied: *also* Alcied; Alkied up

Alky soaked

All at sea

All he can hold

All in

All keyhole

All-overish

All sails set: *also* All sails spread; Under full sail

All schnozzled: *also* All schnozzled up

All shucked up

All there

Altogether: *also* Altogetherly

Ambushed

Amiably incandescent

Amuck

Anchored in sot's bay: *also* Moored in sot's bay

Anesthesized

Angel-altogether

Animated

Ankled

Annihilated

Antifreezed

Antiseptic

➤ **APE**: also Aped; Ape drunk

Apple palsy

Arf an' arf

Arfarfanark

Arsefaced

Arseholed: *also* Arse-holed; Arseholes

As good conditioned as a puppy: One of the odder findings in Lester V. Berrey and Melvin Van den Bark's 1953 *The American Thesaurus Of Slang; A Complete Reference Book Of Colloquial Speech*.

As great as a lord

As wise as Solomon

APE

Asotus

Ass backwards: *also* Ass on backwards

Assed up

At ease: *also* At one's ease

At peace with the floor

At rest

At rights

A-tappin' the bottle

Ate the dog

Awash: *also* Deck awash; decks awash

Away wi' it

Away with the airies

Away with the band

Away with the birds

Away with the pixies

Awry

Awry-eyed

[B]

Baaaaaaaaaaaaa

Baccanalian: Noah Webster lists in first two dictionaries from 1806 and 1828.

Bacchi plenus

Bacchus-bulged

Bacchus-butted

Back home

Back teeth afloat: *also* Back teeth well afloat; Got the back teeth well afloat

Back-assward

Backlamped

Backwards

Badgered

Bagged: *also* Half-bagged; Half in the bag; Has a bag on; In the bag; Shitbagged

Baked

Balearicsed

Ball-dozed

Balmy

Baltic: "The best words conceal stories," Victoria Moore wrote in the *New Statesman* for June 17, 2002: "When asked why she reserved the word Baltic for people who were really, really drunk, a friend's Scottish grandmother explained that

BAZOOKA'D

it was a reflection on the activities of seafaring men from the Moray Firth, who drank to excess in the overseas ports—and sometimes on the boats—while on fishing trips in the Baltic Sea."

Bamboozled

Bang through the elephant

Banged-up

Banjaxed

Banjoed: *also* Banjo'd: "British slang meaning completely drunk, or stoned, under the influence of drugs. It is probably a corruption of 'banjaxed,' an Irish word meaning totally overcome." This from *The London Times* of April 7, 2007.

Baptized

Bar kissing

Barfelnugen

Barleysick

Barmy

Barrel fever

Barreled: *also* Barreled-up; Barreled up; Getting barreled up; Got barreled up

Barrelhouse

Barrelhouse drunk

Barryed

Bashed

Bassackwards

Basted

Bats: *also* Seeing bats

Batted

Battered

Batty

Bazeracked

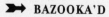 **BAZOOKA'D**

Bazookaed out of my endo

Beaked

Beargered: *also* Be-argered: Defined in *The Slang Dictionary or The Vulgar Words, Street Phrases and "Fast" Expressions of High and Low Society* (London, 1884) as a term for a more intense state of beastliness that comes beyond mild intoxication and before total fuddlement.

Bearing the ensign: *also* Flying the ensign

Beastly drunk: *also* Drunk as a beast: Extreme intoxication. *The Derby Mercury*, May 29, 1872, describes a French woman driving her husband home "...lying in the bottom of the cart like a dead pig—as they say drunk as a beast; which a beast never is, nor consents to be."

Bebado: Drunk to Brazilians, and also the name of a Glasgow bar.

Been among the Philippines: Perhaps a version of the next entry uttered under the influence.

Been among the Philistines

Been at an Indian Feast

Been at Barbados: *also* Been to Barbados: One of Benjamin Franklin's terms and an allusion to the Caribbean island that supplied the bulk of America's rum.

Been at Geneva

Been at the Bibbing Plot: *also* Been in the bibbing plot

Been before George

Been in a storm

Been in the crown office

Been seeing Doctor Brown: Especially in regard to brown ale.

Been seeing doctor bottle

Been to a funeral

Been to France

Been to Jericho
Been to Mexico: *also* Gone to Mexico; In Mexico; Off to Mexico
Been to Olympus: *also* Gone to Olympus; Up on Olympus
Been to the Salt Water: *also* Been to the saltwater
Been too free
Been too free with Sir John Strawberry
Been too free with the creature
Been with Sir John Goa
Beered & shot
Beered up
Beer-gogglin'
Beerified
Beer-soaked
Beery: Listed in *The Slang Dictionary or The Vulgar Words, Street Phrases and "Fast" Expressions of High and Low Society* (London, 1884) as a term for mild intoxication.
Beery-eyed
Befuggered
Beginning to fly
Behind the cork
Belligerent: *also* Belligerant: A term for a state of angry drunkenness, a blend of bellerigent + rant.
Belly up
Below the mahogany
Belted
Belted the grape: To imbibe heavily; to get drunk; to get a buzz on. "Belt," an obsolete slang verb meaning "swallow," was popular in the mid-19th century. As part of the US slang phrase "belt the grape," it again gained currency in the 1930s. "Grape" usually refers to wine but can be used loosely to mean any alcoholic beverage. "Jack takes to belting the old grape

right freely to get his zing back," writes Damon Runyon in *Guys and Dolls*, back in 1931.

Beltered

Bemused: A term for mild intoxication.

Bending over

Bent

Bent an elbow: also Bent his elbow

Bent and broken

Bent out of shape: *also* Half bent out of shape; Twisted out of shape

Bernard Langered: Langer is a German professional golfer and his name's connection to drunkenness is obscure. "Where does this come from?" asked Victoria Moore in her June 17, 2002, article on terms for drunk in the *New Statesman*. "Well, apparently, 'langer' also means penis—probably a corruption of 'long one'—so we're back to boys'-night-out vocabulary again."

Duncan Lamont, a media lawyer at Charles Russell Solicitors, who wrote on these eponymous terms in the February 28, 2003, issue of the *Press Gazette* magazine said, "The good news for lawyers is that the wonderfully complicated English language can free up new defamatory meanings where none were expected (and intention is no defence). According to a BBC compilation there are 141 words for 'drunk' including 'minging,' 'mullered to,' (oddly) 'Bernard Langered,' 'Chevy Chased' and 'Michael Fished!' So no need for old styles of attack such as drunk as a lord."

Beschmuddled

Beside his reckoning

Besoffen: German term which has morphed into the next entry

Besoppen

Besot

Besotted

Bet one's kettle: *also* **Has bet his kettle; Has het his kettle**

Better if he's gone twice after the same load

➤ **BETTY BOOPED**

Betty Ford-ed

Beved up

BETTY BOOPED

Beviedile he avin'
Bevvied
Bewildered
Bewitch'd
Bewottled
Beyond salvage
Beyond the fringe
Bezopen: Flemish
Bezzled

BIT BY A FOX

Bibacious

Bibulous

Biffed

Biffy

Biggy

Binged: *also* Binged up; On a binge; With a binge on

Bingoed: *also* Bingoe: In *Blackguardiana*, 1794, bingo is a cant word for brandy.

Bird-eyed

Birlin: *also* Burlin

Bit

➤ BIT BY A FOX

Bit his grannan: *also* Biting one's grannam: The term is an old slang term for grandam—literally "great lady"—defined as such in the 1811 version of *Dictionary of the Vulgar Tongue*.

Biting one's name in: *also* Bit his name in

Biting the brute: *also* Bite in the brute

Biting them off

Black jacked

Blacked out

Blacken'd

Blackout drive

Bladdered: Defined by Julian Champkin of the *London Daily Mail*, October 25, 2001: "'I was right royally bladdered,' said the Cardiff accountant whose millennium night celebrations were so lively that he had to take out newspaper advertisements to apologise to people he'd offended. It means 'drunk' and is derived from beer's effect on the bladder."

Blanked

Blasé

Blasted: *also* Under a blast

Blathered

Blatted

Blazed: 19th-century bartender Jerry Thomas invented a number of drinks including the Tom & Jerry (a rearrangement of his name) and the flaming, airborne Blue Blazer. When U.S. Grant saw Thomas create one of these he awarded him a box of cigars.

Blazing drunk

Blazing fou'

Blazooed

Bleary

Bleary-eyed: *also* Getting bleary-eyed; Got bleary-eyed

Bleezin: *also* Bleezin'; Bleezin fou

Blended

Blewed

Blighted

Blimped

Blind: *also* Blind drunk; Blind, staggerin' drunk; Blinded; Get blind; Half-blind; Stone blind; Stoney blind

Blind staggers: *also* Got the blind staggers: Bob Skole who served with the 7th Cavalry recalled correctly that this is also an animal disease commonly affecting horses, in which the animal walks with an unsteady, staggering gait and seems to be blind.

Blinders

Blindo

Blinking drunk

Blinky

Blissed: *also* Blissed out

Blistered

Blit

Blithered

Blithero

Blittered

Blitzed: *also* Blitzed out

Blitzkrieged

Bloated

Blobbin'

Block and block

Blocked

Bloody drunk: Bloody is used as an expletive in such phrases as "a bloody fool," "bloody drunk," etc., and arose from associating folly and drunkenness, etc., with what are called "bloods," or aristocratic rowdies. Similar to "drunk as a lord," explains *Brewer's Dictionary of Phrase and Fable*, 1898. In his 1828 dictionary Noah Webster affixes the label "very vulgar" to the use of bloody and gives "bloody drunk" as an example.

Blootered

Blottered

Blotto: *also* Blotto'd; Blottoed; Got blotto; Mug blotto:
If this term was not coined by P.G. Wodehouse, it was popularized by him. In an interview which appeared in the *New York World* of March 22, 1922, he cites it as an improvement over American terms like "stewed." "Blotto" is the ultimate stage of inebriation in Edmund Wilson's 1927 "Lexicon of Prohibition." A line from *The Simpsons* is, "My name is Otto, I like to get blotto." Merriam-Webster gives 1917 as date of origin.

Blowed: *also* Blowed-away

Blowin' a

Blowin' beer bubbles

Blowing

Blown: *also* Blown away; Blown out; Blown over; Blown up;

Blown-away

Blowzy: *also* Blowzy blue

Bludgeoned by life

Blue

Blue around the gills

Blue blind bleezin drunk

Blued: "The Blue Ruin" was a term for brandy recorded as early as 1845, in *The Satirist; or, the Censor of the Times*, December 7, 1845.

Blue-eyed

Bluttered

Boggled

Boggy

Boiled

Boiled as an owl

Boiled out of shape

Boiled to the gills: John Ayto notes the prevalence of cooking terms in speaking of excessive boozing—as in "fried," "boiled," "steamed." There's "pickled," as well, from the early 19th century. *Oxford English Dictionary* dates "boiled" as slang for "drunk" to 1885.

Boiling drunk

Boinked

Bollixed

Bollock-eyed

Bolloxed: Irish

Bombarded

Bomb-boozled

Bombed: *also* Bombed out of his mind; Bombed out of their kugs

Boned

Bongo: *also* Bongoed

Bonkered: *also* Bonkers

Boofy

Boogaloo

Boogered up

Boosed

Booze blind

Boozed: *also* Boozed-up; Boozed up; Getting boozed up

Boozed as the gage: *also* Booz'd the Gage

Boozified

Boozing

Boozington

Boozy: *also* Boosy; Boozie; Boozy-woozy; Getting a little boozy; Getting boozy; Looks boozy

Boracho: *also* Borracho: from the Spanish, adopted by English as early as 1828 when Noah Webster lists the derivative "borachio" as a term meaning "drunkard."

Boris Yeltsin: *also* Boris Yeltsinned: After the notoriously alcoholic Russian Prime Minister Boris Yeltsin. On a classic episode of "The Simpsons," they gave a breathalyzer to patrons in the bar to determine if it was safe for them to drive. The meter from lowest to highest had the following degrees of inebriation: Not drunk/Tipsy/Pissed/Boris Yeltsin.

Bosco absoluto

Boshy

Bosky: *also* A touch of boskiness: When Jack Smith, longtime columnist for the *Los Angeles Times* noted in an article from September 29, 1981, that his favorite word was "bosky," meaning "wooded or sylvan in the sense of a 'bosky dell,' he was quickly informed by a woman who wrote "Regency Romances" that, according to *The Penguin Dictionary of Historical Slang*, bosky is defined as "dazed, or fuddled; mildly drunk" and that many of the "young nobles in Regencies are often a trifle bosky." Smith's reaction was to like it all the more and it stood as his favorite word. It is an older term defined in *The*

*Slang Dictionary or The Vulgar Words, Street Phrases and "Fast"
Expressions of High and Low Society* (London, 1884) as a term
for mild intoxication.

Both eyes in one socket

Bottled: *also* Well bottled; Well-bottled

Bottle-ached

Bottle-knocked into a cocked hat

Bottlestruck

Bottle-suckered

Bourbon-eyed

Bourboned

Bought the black sun

Bowzed: *also* Bowz'd

Bowzered

Boxed: *also* Boxed out; Boxed up

Brahms and Lizst: *also* Brahms; Franz Liszt; Mozart and Liszt:
Cockney rhyming slang for "pissed." Quotation: "Unless you can
get Brahms on 21 units, you've come to the wrong place." from
the *London Sun*, March 21, 1994. There is also a pub in London
with this name.

Brained

Brandy-faced

Brannigan

Breaky leg

Breath strong enough to carry coal with

Breezy

Brewed

Brick in his hat: *also* A brick in the hat; Has a brick in his hat:
"Her husband had taken to the tavern, and often came home
very late 'with a brick in his hat.'" —Henry W. Longfellow,
"Kavanagh," 1849. An interesting explanation, attributed to

one Timothy W. Robinson of Morrill, Maine, appears in the April, 1948, issue of *American Speech*: "Then they (matches) were made so that one using them had to have a brick to scratch them on, and the saying was that he carried a brick in his hat, so when anyone had been to the store and walked a little crooked, the boys would say 'he had a brick in his hat.'"

Bricked

Bridgey

Bright-eyed: *also* Bright in the eye

Broken

Bruised

Brutify'd: A term which Benjamin Franklin did not include in his list but mentioned in a postscript. "I do not doubt but that there are many more in use; and I was even tempted to add a new one my self under the Letter B, to wit, *Brutify'd*. But upon Consideration, I fear'd being guilty of Injustice to the Brute Creation, if I represented Drunkenness as a beastly Vice, since, 'tis well-known, that the Brutes are in general a very sober sort of People." *The Pennsylvania Gazette*, January 13, 1736/7.

Bubbed

Bubbled

Bubby

Bucked up

Bucket is crackers

Buckled: Irish

Budgey: *also* Budgy

Buffy: Listed in *The Slang Dictionary or The Vulgar Words, Street Phrases and "Fast" Expressions of High and Low Society* (London, 1884) as a term for mild intoxication.

Bug-eyed

Bugged

Buggered

Buicked

Bulge

Bull-dozed: One of the many findings of Ernest L. Abel in his 1987 *Alcohol: Wordlore and Folklore* is that this term derives from bull, which meant to water down liquor. It shows up in phrases like "bull the cask" which meant to fill an empty rum cask with water and draw out the alcohol which had seeped into the wood to produce an intoxicating drink.

Bullaphants: Irish slang for "drunk." It derives from the (originally Cockney) slang "elephants," which is itself the abbreviated form of "elephant's trunk" rhyming slang for "totally drunk."

Bullet

➤ **BULLETPROOF:** *also* Bulletproofed

Bumfuzzled

Bummed: *also* Bummed out

Bumpsie: *also* Bumpsy

Bun: *also* Bunned; Bunnied; Got a bun on; Had a bun on; Has a bun on; With a bun on: As in "to have a bun on." Probably stems from the next entry: bung.

Bung: *also* Bung-full; Bunged; Full to the bung; Got bunged

Bung-eyed: *also* Bung'd his eye

Bungfu

Bungie: *also* Bungey; Bungy

Bungay fair

Buoyant

Buoyed

Burdocked: *also* Burdock'd

Burgled

Buried: The penultimate condition of drunkenness, followed by "blotto," in Edmund Wilson's 1927 hierarchy of terms.

Burned to the ground

Burns with a low blue flame: This almost certainly has some relationship to the ancient assertion that if one drank enough rum or brandy and was bled, the blood would burn blue until

BULLET PROOF

totally consumed. As early as 1836 this belief was satirized, which probably helped the idea to remain current. "The doctrine of the spontaneous combustion of drunkards has just been exemplified in New York, in the case of a man who had drunk two gallons of rum in five days; he was afterwards bled, and on the application of a match, the blood took light, and burnt blue until it was consumed. Spirit-drinkers should be warned by this, that they may, by possibility, 'flare up' without bargaining for such a luxury," read a dispatch published in *The Satirist, and the Censor of the Time*, March 6, 1836.

Burnt

Burst

Busheled

Business on both sides of the way

Busky: *also* Buskey

Busted: *also* Busted up; On a bust; On the bust

Butt wasted

Buttered

Butt-faced

Buttoned

Buzzed: *also* A-buzz; Abuzz; Buzzed up; Got a buzz on; Has a buzz; Slightly buzzed

Buzzy: *also* Buzzey

[C]

Cabbaged

Cached

Caged

Cagrin'd

Caked

Called the wharf cat

Canceled

Candy

Canned: *also* Canned up; Half-canned; Shitcanned

Cannon: *also* Drunker than a cannon; Got cannon

Canon

Can't bit his thumb

Can't find his ass with both hands

Can't hit the ground with his hat

Can't hit your ass with both hands

Can't say *National Intelligencer*: This is the name of a newspaper published in Washington, DC, from about 1800 to 1867.

Can't see a hole in a ladder: *also* Can't see through a ladder; Not able to see through a ladder: This term appears in *The Slang Dictionary or The Vulgar Words, Street Phrases and "Fast" Expressions of High and Low Society* (London, 1884) as a term for the most intense state of drunkeness.

Can't sport a right light

Can't walk a chalk line

Capable

Capernoited: *also* Capernoitie

Capped off

Cap-sick

Captained

Cargoed

Carrying a heavy load

Carrying the dark dog on his back

Carrying two red lights

Carvered

Cased

Cast

Castaway

Casters up

Casting up his accounts

Cat

Catched: *also* Catch'd

Catching a heat

Catsood: Corruption of the French *quatre sous,* or four sous, the price of a drink during the early days of World War I. The price was later raised but the term remained the same without regard to price, as explained in *Soldier and Sailor Words & Phrases,* 1925.

Caught

Caught off his hobbyhorse

Caught the Irish flu

Certified drunk

Chagrined: *also* Chagrin'd

Chap-fallen: *also* Chapfallen

Charged: *also* Getting charged up; Got charged-up; Super-charged

Chateaued

Cheary

Chemically enhanced

Chemically imbalanced

Chemically inconvenienced: From a "Polically Correct Guide" circulating on the Internet: "She does not get DRUNK or TIPSY—she gets CHEMICALLY INCONVENIENCED."

Cherry Merry: *also,* Cherry-merry

Cherubimical

Chevy Chased: From a BBC compilation of March, 2002, possibly rhyming slang for "shit-faced."

Chickery

Chinny

Chipper

Chippit

Chirping-merry

Chloroformed: From New York café owner Roland Elliot's 1913 collection, a term meaning completely drunk.

Chock-a-block

Chocked

Choked

Chootled

Chopped

Chuck full

Chucked

Circling over Shannon: In Ireland, "Circling Over Shannon" is a euphemism for being drunk, coined after Boris Yeltsin's infamous 1994 trip to Ireland where he was reportedly too drunk to get off the plane, so they circled the Shannon airport six times before landing to sober him up.

Clattere

Clear: *also* Clear out: In the *Oxford English Dictionary* it is listed as the 24th meaning of the word as "*slang*. Very drunk. *Obs.*" The term "clearly" had application to easy victims of crime. James Caulfield's *Blackguardiana* (1794) defines CLEAR as "very drunk. The cull is clear, let's bite him; the fellow is very drunk, let's cheat him."

Clinched

Clinked up

Clipped the King's English: *also* Clipp'd the King's English; He Clips the King's English

Clobbered: *also* Really clobbered; Slightly clobbered

Clobstered

Coagulated

Coarse

Cocido

Cocked: *also* Cock'd; Full-cocked; Half-cocked; Majorly

cocked: *Blackguardiana*, 1794, lists "COCK ALE, a provoca-
tive drink." The ale in question was brewed with minced cock
(rooster) and was one of several ales made with meat. There
are a number of pubs in the British Isles which are named
"The Cock" or have the image of a cock on the pub sign,
which was once a signal that the establishment featured cock-
fighting in its courtyard. According to his *Diary*, Samuel Pepys
frequented a tavern called "the Cock ale-house." There are
several possible etymologies for the word "cocktail" of which
one is that it comes from the term "cock ale."

Cocked as a log

Cocked off your ass

Cocked to the gills

Cockeyed: *also* Cock eyed; Cock-eyed; Cockeyed drunk; Half-
cockeyed

Cognaceyed

Cognacked

Coguey: a dram of any spirituous liquor is a "cogue."

Coguy

Cogy: *also* Cogey

Cold comboozelated

Colored

Colt 45'd

Comblasted

Comblinded

Comboozelated

Comboozled

Come home by the villages: "To Express the Condition of
45 on a Merry Pin," *New London Gazette*, December 13, 1771:
"This is provincial: when a man comes home by the fields he
meets nobody, consequently is sober; when he comes home
by the Villages, he calls first at one house, then another and

drinks at all."

Comfortable

Comin': *also* Comin' on; Commin', Commin' on

Commencin': *also* Commencin' to feel it

Commode-hugging drunk

Concerned: also Concern'd

Conflummoxed

Conked: *also* Conked out

Consumed a rancid oyster

Cooked

Cookin' with gas

Cootered

Copacetic: *also* Copasetic: "Copacetic" is the preferred spelling in both the *Oxford English Dictionary* and *Merriam-Webster's Collegiate Dictionary*. The term means "very satisfied" and has long been associated with jazz, especially the jazz artist Dizzy Gillespie.

Copped a crane

Cop-sluggin' drunk

Cork high and bottle deep

Corked: *also* Corked-up

Corkneyed: A play on "corkney" which is a double pun on "Cockney" and "cork," alluding to supposed Cockney drinking habits.

Corkscrewed

Corky

Corned: *also* Corned up; Half-corned; Well corned; Well-corned: In *The American Language* (1921), H.L. Mencken notes that this is probably an Americanism derived from "corn-whiskey" or "corn-juice." John Russell Bartlett in his *Dictionary Of Americanisms* (1848) terms it an Americanism but adds that it is used in the same sense in England. It

COUNT DRUNKULA

appears in *The Slang Dictionary or The Vulgar Words, Street Phrases and "Fast" Expressions of High and Low Society* (London, 1884) as a term for mild intoxication. An early American example: "William McG. brought a load of corn to market, and got corned on the strength of it." From the *Daily Pennant*, St. Louis, May 27, 1840.

Cornered

Corroded

➤ **COUNT DRUNKULA:** A play on the fictional vampire Count Dracula and the chocolate-flavored breakfast cereal Count Chocula.

Coxy-foxy

Cracked: *also* Crack'd

Crackling

Cramped: *also* Cramp'd

Cranked

Cranky

Crapped: *also* Crapped out

Crappers

Crapulous: Noah Webster defined this in his 1828 *Dictionary*: "Drunk; surcharged with liquor; sick by intemperance."

Crashed

Crashed and burned

Crazed

Crazy

Crazy drunk

Crazy-legged

Creamed

Croaked

Crocked: *also* Getting crocked; half-crocked

Crocko

Crocus

Cronk

Crooked

Crooking the elbow

Crop sick: *also* Cropsick

Crop stricken

Cross-eyed

Crossed the Ruby: i.e. to have crossed the Rubicon, meaning to have drunk too much and passed out. An article in the *Brooklyn Eagle* of December 16, 1934, entitled "Slang in the Days of David Copperfield" reports that this was the slang of the "dandies and literati" in the Copperfield era.

Cruckooed

Crump

Crump fooled

Crump footed

Crumped: *also* Crumped out

Crumpled

Crunk: Crazy + drunk, as per the Urban Dictionary, a web-based dictionary of slang, which also contains this amplification posted by a contributor identified as Ishkur: "In 1995, Conan O'Brien and Andy Richter were scheming ways to get past the TV censors on Conan's late night talk show, and they settled on an all-purpose, suitable replacement for the infamous seven dirty swearwords that they couldn't say on TV: crunk. The choice to use that word was definitely not random. Ice T just happened to be on the show that night, and he likely fed the word to them beforehand and certainly helped fuel its popularity during the telecast. ("That was seriously crunked up, right there.") But Ice never claimed to have come up with the word—he probably got it from dirty south rappers, who had been using it for years as a euphemism for getting re-

ally crazy and fucked up on marijuana and alcohol (stoned
and drunk. Chronic plus drunk = crunk). Or maybe crack and
drunk. Or coke and drunk. Or maybe just being crazy and
drunk. Whatever it is, it means getting really crazy and fucked
up." Another Urban Dictionary contributor adds "originally
coined by Dr. Seuss in 1972, in his book *Marvin K. Mooney Will
You Please Go Now!*: "You can go in a crunk-car if you wish."

Crunk as a cooter

Crushed

Crying drunk

Crying jag

Cuckooed

Cued up

Cupped

Cup-shot: *also* Cupshotten

Cup stricken

Curbed

Curious

Curried and mashed

Curved, *also* Curv'd

Cushed

Cut: *also* Deep cut; Got cut; Half cut; Half-cut; Terribly cut:
Blackguardiana, 1794, says "CUT. Drunk, a little cut over the
head, slightly intoxicated; to cut, to leave a person or compa-
ny, to cut up well, to die rich." Found in Benjamin Franklin's
"The Drinker's Dictionary," and cited in *The Slang Dictionary
or The Vulgar Words, Street Phrases and "Fast" Expressions of High
and Low Society* (London, 1884) as a term for a more intense
state of beastliness that comes beyond mild intoxication and
before total intoxication.

Cut in the craw

[D]

D&D: Drunk and disorderly. H.L. Mencken in *The American Language* insists that this is an Americanism along with "... "T. B." (for "tuberculosis"), "G. B." (for "grand bounce"), "23," "on the Q.T.," "f.o.b.," and the army verb, "to go a.w.o.l." (to be absent without leave). The language breeds such short forms of speech prodigiously; every trade and profession has a host of them; they are innumerable in the slang of sport. Often they represent the end-products of terms long in decay, e.g., elevated railway: elevated: el: L."

D.T.'s (delirium tremens)

DAFFY WITH BOOZE

DUI'ed

Dacked!

Daffy

➤ **DAFFY WITH BOOZE**

Daffy with moonshine

Daffy with mountain dew

Daffy with sentimental water

Dagged: *also* Dagg'd

Damaged

Damp

Daquifried

Dark day with him

Dead drunk: *also* Laying out dead drunk: So intoxicated as to be wholly powerless. Used by Shakespeare, as in this exchange in *Othello*, Act II, Scene iii:

> CASSIO: Is your Englishman so expert in his drinking?
>
> IAGO: Why, he drinks you with facility your Dane dead drunk; he sweats not to overthrow your Almain; he gives your Hollander a vomit ere the next pottle can be filled.
>
> CASSIO: To the health of our general!

"Pythagoras has finely observed that a man is not to be considered dead drunk till he lies on the floor and stretches out his arms and legs to prevent his going lower." —C.S. Warren, *Brewer's Dictionary of Phrase and Fable*, 1898.

Dead to the world: *also* Out to the world

Dead 'un

Dead-oh: *also* Dead-oh!

Dean Martoonied: A blend of Dean Martin + martooni (martini in slurred speech). Martin's show business persona was that of a drunk:

"Dean, why do you drink so much?"

"I drink to forget."

"What're trying to forget?"

"I dunno, I've forgotten."

Debacled

Debauched

Decandently drunk: Overheard by a woman talking on her cell phone in Boston: "He was decadently drunk … I don't know what is with him."

Decanted

Decayed

Decimated

Decks aflush

Deep cut

Deep drunk

DEFCON 1: Defense Readiness Condition, term for the readiness of the Armed Forces in the United States. DEFCON 1 represents expectation of actual imminent attack, and is not known to have ever been declared.

Deformed

Deleerit

Demented

Demoralized

Denatured

De-ossified

Derailed

Destroyed

Detained on business

Dew drunk

Dewed

Diced

Did the job up right

Diddled

Ding swizzled: *also* Ding-swizzled

Dinged: *also* Dinged out; Dinged up; Dinged-out

Dingleberried

Dingy

Dinky

Dipped

Dipped his beak

Dipped his bill

Dipped in the wassail bowl

Dipped rather deep: *also* Dipped too deep; Dipping rather deep

Dippy: From New York café owner Roland Elliot's 1913 collection, term for moderately drunk.

Dipsy

Dirtfaced

Dirty drunk

Discombobulated

Discomboobulated

Discouraged

Discumfuddled

Disguised: *also* Disguiz'd

Disgusting

Disorderly

Distinguished

Dithered

Dizzy: *also* Feeling dizzy

Dizzy as a coot

Dizzy as a goose: *also* As dizzy as a goose

Dizzydone

Dlinkadik: From the Volapuk language, it has been said it sounds like pidgin English and had a moment of fashion. *The Milwaukee Sentinel*, August 20, 1888, wrote: "It would be quite as disgraceful for a man to be seen 'reeling home dlinkadik' as it would be to be seen 'staggering home drunk.'"

Dog drunk: Very drunk

Dog-sucking drunk: This may be a contribution to the language from author Carl Hiassen. In *Double Whammy*, he writes: "On the night of January 15, Dickie Lockhart got dog-sucking drunk on Bourbon Street and was booted out of a topless joint for tossing rubber nightcrawlers on the dancers."

Doing the emperor

Doing the lord

Done a Falstaff

Done a vanishing act

Done an Archie

Done got out

Done over

Done up

Doped: *also* Doped over; Getting dopy; Half-doped

Dork faced

Dot Cottoned: Dot Cotton is the name of a chain-smoking character on the British soap *East/Enders*.

Dotted

Dotty

Double up

Double Tongu'd

Double-headed

Down

Down and out

Down for the count

Down the creek

Down the drain: *also* In the drain

Down with barrel fever

➡ DOWN WITH THE FISH: *also:* Drunk with the fish

Down with the blue devils
Dragging his bottom
Dragging the load
Dramling
Drank

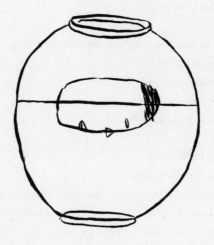

DOWN WITH THE FISH

Draped: *also* Slightly draped

Draw a blank

Drenched

Dribbly

Drinkative

Drinky

Dripped to the tits

Dripping: *also* Adrip; Dripping tight

Drita: Norwegian

Driving home 'cause I can't fucking walk

Driving the brewer's horse

Dronken

Drop in the eye: *also* A drop in the eye; Got a drop in his eye; Has a drop in his eye

Drove the big white bus

Drove the brewer's horse

Drove the porcelain bus

Drowned

Drowning brain cells

Drowning the shamrock

Drowsy: Employed in the 2006 Broadway musical "The Drowsy Chaperone," in which the term was identified as slang for "drunk" in the 1920s, which is when the show was set. The joke in the show is that the chaperone has had too much to drink and keeps saying she's "drowsy." One reviewer termed it "the worst title ever."

Drucking funk

Druck-steaming

Drunje: Beyond drunk, according the Urban Dictionary website.

Drunk: *also* About drunk; About half-drunk; All drunked up; Feeling drunk; Full drunk; Getting all over drunk; Half-drunk; Just about drunk; Just about half-drunk; On a drunk; On the drunk; Plenty drunk; Pretty drunk; Real drunk; Slightly drunk; Thoroughly drunk; Totally drunk; Very drunk: The late Chicago baseball announcer Harry Caray refused to use the word, using terms like "blind" or "smashed" instead. He told Steve Bogira of the *Chicago Tribune* in 1979, "I don't use drunk. Maybe there is something negative about it."

Drunk and disorderly: Long established term used by law enforcement. A trial for pickpocketing at the Old Bailey in London on June 11, 1829, contains this bit of testimony: "I had seen McDougall about Christmas last, when he came upon my beat drunk and disorderly."

Drunk and down

Drunk and riotous

Drunk as ten Indians

Drunk as a badger

Drunk as a barroom rag

Drunk as a bastard

Drunk as a bat

Drunk as a beggar

Drunk as a besom

Drunk as a bicycle

Drunk as a bunch of Japanese students at night under cherry blossoms: Culled from a review of a Japanese restaurant by Vanessa Woods in *The Sydney Morning Herald*, March 8, 2008: "We continue eating our sushi, thinking maybe the prawns are some kind of Japanese decoration, like a goldfish bowl. By the time we finish, the sherry is gone and the prawns are as drunk as a bunch of Japanese students at night under cherry blossoms."

Drunk as a brewer's fart

Drunk as a broken cart-wheel

Drunk as a bunghole

Drunk as a coon

Drunk as a coon hunter

Drunk as a coon on stump-likker

Drunk as a cook

Drunk as a coot

Drunk as a cootie

Drunk as a dog

Drunk as a drowned mouse

Drunk as a fart

Drunk as a fiddler: The reference is to the fiddler at wakes, fairs, and on board ship, who used to be paid in liquor for playing to rustic dancers, from *Brewer's Dictionary of Phrase and Fable*, 1898.

Drunk as a fiddler's bitch

Drunk as a fish: *also* Drunk as a kettlefish: The allusion is to the way many fish swim with their mouths open, thus seeming to drink continuously. This popular simile is usually used to describe a drinker with an extraordinary capacity to put away liquor. Ben Johnson used this term, among others.

Drunk as a fishup: James Joyce uses this in *Finnegans Wake*.

Drunk as a fly

Drunk as a fool: A popular drunken simile during the Civil War according to John D. Wright in his *Language of the Civil War*.

Drunk as a four-dollar shotgun in Missouri

Drunk as a fowl

Drunk as a Gosport fiddler

Drunk as a handcart: *also* Drunk as a hand cart

Drunk as a hillbilly at a rooster fight

Drunk as a king

Drunk as a little red wagon

Drunk as a log

Drunk as a loon

Drunk as a lord: Comparison which appears as early as 1775
(*Morning Chronicle and London Advertiser*) in which a soldier
about to go to America to fight in the Revolution confessed:
"I was drunk as a lord when I enlisted, but I little thought that
the once honorable profession of soldier was to be obsequious
to every dirty duty the influence of authority could impose…"

Brewer's *Dictionary of Phrase and Fable*, 1898, commented:
"Before the great temperance movement set in, in the lat-
ter half of the nineteenth century, those who could afford to
drink thought it quite *comme il faut* to drink two, three, or
even more bottles of port wine for dinner, and few dinners
ended without placing the guests under the table in a hopeless
state of intoxication. The temperate habits of the last quarter
of the nineteenth century render this phrase now almost un-
intelligible."

Fyodor Dostoyevsky, in *The House of the Dead* : "Then
vodka was brought out; the hero of the day would get drunk as
a lord and always walked all over the prison, reeling and staggering, trying to show to everyone that he was drunk, that he
was "jolly" and so deserving of general respect." Everywhere
among the Russian people a certain sympathy was felt for a
drunken man; in prison he was positively treated with respect. The comparison is still very much at play and is even,
on occasion, still applied to lords, as in this description of
the House of Lords by Brian Reade in *The Daily Mirror*, July
23, 1998. "Chaps who can turn up to the House as drunk as a
Lord after a three-hour lunch at their club, register their at-
tendance, then go back to their club or simply fall asleep in
the Chamber."

From Edwin Radford's *Unusual Words And How They Came
About*, Philosophical Library, 1946, Page 57: "When George

III was King and, indeed, for long afterwards, drinking was the sign of the gentleman! To be as drunk as a lord was a sure mark of gentility. A 'three bottle man' was a pattern of society. Few dinners but ended with all the guests helpless under the table in front of the chairs upon which they had been sitting. The temperance movement which set in towards the end of the nineteenth century put an end to heavy drinking."

Drunk as a monkey: *also* Drunker than a monkey: F. Scott Fitzgerald writes in *The Great Gatsby* that on her wedding day, Daisy Buchanan is found "lying on her bed as lovely as the June night in her flowered dress—and as drunk as a monkey," holding in her hand a letter from her former lover.

Drunk as a mook

Drunk as a mouse: *also* Drunk as mice: This is a very early usage, which pre-dates Chaucer according to *The Oxford Dictionary of English Proverbs* of 1935: a. 1310 in WRIGHT *Lyric P.* xxxix. 111. "When that he is dronke as ase a dreynt mous, thenne we shule borewe the wed ate bayly."

Drunk as a mule

Drunk as a newt

Drunk as a perraner: A perraner is an eponomous name for a tinner or tinsmith, from St. Perran, the patron saint of the trade. The comparison arises from the tale that when the Saint discovered tin there was great feasting and celebration among those with a new trade; hence "drunk as a perraner." The discovery took place when the holy man built a cooking fire using a heavy black stone as one side of the fireplace, and when it got extremely hot, it yielded a stream of brilliant white metal. This etymology appeared in *The American Architect and Building News*, March 14, 1903.

Drunk as a pig

Drunk as a piss ant: *also* Drunk as a waltzing pissant; Drunker than a waltzing puissant; Pissant-drunk

Drunk as a poet: *also* Drunk as a poet on payday: This phrase got a boost from "The Simpsons" TV show, where Marge says to Homer: "Every time you go to that cook-off you get drunk as a poet on payday."

Drunk as a polony: The name of a sausage, but this may be a thinly-veiled Polish slur.

Drunk as a prohibition enforcement agent: Coined by Franklin Pierce Adams, a writer for the *New York Tribune*.

Drunk as a possum

Drunk as a rat: *also* Pissed as a rat; Drunker than a shithouse rat: According to the *The Oxford Dictionary of English Proverbs* (Clarendon Press, 1935), this dates to 1553: "As if one had . . . kepte the Tauerne till he had been as dronke as a Ratte."

Drunk as a rolling fart

Drunk as a sailor

Drunk as a ship's cat: Newcastle, England

Drunk as a skunk: *also* Drunk as a skunk in a trunk: This sounds like a very old construction, but the earliest use of the term that the author could find was from the *Los Angeles Times* of September 2, 1963. It was in a column whose author asked what skunks drank to get drunk.

Drunk as a soot

Drunk as a sow: *also* Drunk as a peach orchard sow; Drunk as David's Sow; Drunk as Davy's Sow: Extremely drunk or inebriated. According to Grose's *Classical Dictionary Of The Vulgar Tongue* (1785), this expression arose from the following circumstances. A pub keeper in Hereford, David Lloyd, had a sow with six legs which he kept on public display. One day, after his wife had imbibed a bit too heavily, she retired to the pig sty to sleep it off. To some customers he brought out to see his porcine oddity, Davy exclaimed, "There is a sow for you! Did you ever see the like?" Whereupon one viewer replied, "Well, it's the drunkest sow I ever beheld." From that day, Mr. Lloyd's wife was known as Davy's sow. The expression has been in use since about 1670, sometimes in the form "drunk as David's sow."

Drunk as a tapster

Drunk as a tick

Drunk as a tinker

Drunk as a top

Drunk as a wheel: From *Fun*, a London magazine of humor and satire, on October 3, 1893: "Drunk as a Wheel," a poem with this final stanza:

> *If a man is "screwed" and "t(y)red,"*
> *And he's rolling home bemired—*
> *Though, perhaps, it's too colloqially put—*
> *His movement will reveal*
> *He's as drunk as any wheel,*
> *When he spins around and tumbles on his "nut."*

Drunk as a wheelbarrow: *also* Drunk as a wheel barrow: A classic from the 17th century; according to the research of William George Smith who edited *The Oxford Dictionary of English Proverbs* (1935) it first appeared in 1694 as: "A . . . sottish Fellow, continually raddled, and as drunk as a Wheelbarrow."

Drunk as an ass

Drunk as an emperor

Drunk as an idiot picking daisies

Drunk as an owl; *also* Drunk as a big owl; Drunk as a biled owl; Drunk as a boiled owl; Drunk as a hoot owl; Drunker than a boiled owl; Drunker than a hoot owl: The question of why an owl was put to Evan Morris on his popular website, word-detective.com. He responded, "As to 'why an owl?' the only possible answer is 'why not?' Nearly every other animal short of penguins has been maligned in this fashion. 'Drunk as a' has been followed by, at various times, pig, fly, fowl, lion, fish, loon, rat, tick, mouse, newt, and, of course, skunk. Again, logic does not loom large in such imagery, but the choice of an owl may have been in reference to the perceived similarity of an owl's wide gaze to a drunk's glassy stare." In any event, the construction is an old and venerable one. As long ago as 1750 Horace Walpole wrote of "sitting guzzling" and getting "drunk as an owl." "Drunk as a boiled owl" is ancient, but also as modern as contemporary writer Molly Ivins, who used it in her *Nothin' But Good Times Ahead*. She also used *spiflicated* in the same work.

Drunk as bacchus

Drunk as ballylana

Drunk as blazes: "Blazes" of course means the devil, according to *Brewer's Dictionary of Phrase and Fable*, 1898.

Drunk as buggery

Drunk as Chloe: *also* Blind as Chloe: Chloe, or rather Cloe, is the cobbler's wife of Linden Grove, to whom the poet Matthew Prior was attached. She was notorious for her drinking habits.

Drunk as coote brown: *also* Drunk as cooter brown; Drunker than Cooter Brown; Drunker than Scootum Brown

Drunk as eight hundred dollars

Drunk as forty billygoats

Drunk as fuck

Drunk as heaven

Drunk as hell: *also* Drunker than hell

Drunk as hoot

Drunk as muck

Drunk as seven earls jumping fences: Term used by Margaret Mitchell in *Gone with the Wind*: "She remembered him

coming home from Charleston and Atlanta laden with gifts
that were never appropriate, remembered too, with a faint
smile through tears, how he came home in the wee hours from
Court Day at Jonesboro, drunk as seven earls jumping fences,
his rollicking voice raised in 'The Wearin' o' the Green.'"

Drunk as the devil

Drunk as whiskey

Drunk as who shot John: *also* Drunker than who shot John

Drunk as Zeus

Drunk clear through

Drunk for sure

Drunk in his dumpes

Drunk like Sinatra

Drunk more than one has bled

Drunk overnight and dry in the morn: 18th century refrain to
ballad "The Answer to the King of the Drunkards." The opening
stanza goes:

> *My name is bold Kelly, a hearty young lad,*
> *And many a hug of the girls I have had.*
> *And tho' I have done it, pray where is the harm,*
> *To be drunk over-night and dry in the morn.*

Drunk till next Sunday

Drunk to the nines

Drunk to the pulp

Drunk uncled

Drunk up

Drunken

Drunker than 300 dollars

Drunker than 700 dollars

Drunker than a fiddler's clerk

Drunker than a nine-high straight

Drunker than a sack of assholes

Drunker than a southern baptist preacher at a high school dance

Drunker than whiskey

Drunkish: In an 1803 calculation of the condition of weekend revelers this is a condition rated after "in high glee," "staggering," "tipsy," "muzzy" and "dead drunk"—hence a condition of not being quite drunk. (From *Weekly Visitor or Ladies' Miscellany*, June 18, 1803.)

Drunkity drunk

Drunkok

Drunksy: According to an entry for this term on the Urban Dictionary website: "Term used to define a specific state of drunkenness. The point between tipsy and drunk. Past tipsy, but not quite drunk yet: 'Half an hour after my glasses of rum, I had 2 shots of Johnnie Walker. I wasn't revealing my deepest secrets to the first person I saw, but I was still having a little trouble focusing on a specific point. I guess I was just drunksy.'"

Drunkulent

Drunky: *also* Drunkey; Drunkie; Drunky drunk: A popular adjective meaning "drunk" during the Civil War, and often used before a name, e.g., "We met drunky Wilson on the road," according to John D. Wright in his *Language of the Civil War*.

Dry

Due for drydock

Dull in the eye

Dull-eyed

Dumbo: Quasi-acronym for Drunken Upper-class Businessman Over the limit.

Dumped

D.W.I.ed (driving while intoxicated)

[E]

Ears ringing: *also* Ears are ringing

Easy

Eat a pudding bagg

➤ **EATIN' DIRT**

Ebriose: *also* Ebrios; Ebrious

Ebrity: From an 18th century dictionary by Dyche and Pardon: "Ebriety: drunkness, a delighting in liquor to excess." It is also listed by Noah Webster in his 1828 *Dictionary*.

Edged; *also* Got an edge on; Has an edge on; On the edge; Over the edge; With an edge on

Effed up

El whappo'd

Electrified

Elephants: *also* All pink elephants; Been elephants; Seeing pink elephants; Seeing the elephants

Elephant's trunk: *also* Elephant's: Cockney/Australian rhyming slang was first recorded in England during the 1850s. In his book *The Lingo: Listening to Australian English*, Graham Seal says it is still commonly used in Australia. "The phrase (originally Cockney) is often abbreviated to 'elephant's' / 'elephants' and is common in the UK, Ireland and Australia," writes Antonio Lillo.

Elevated: *also* State of elevation

Elevated with the juice of the grape: "The manager of the King's Theater...was one Thomas Killigrew, said to be a 'great talker, especially when a little elevated with the juice of the grape,'" from *Nell Gwynn: Mistress to a King* by Charles Beauclerk.

Eliminated

Embalmed

End of the line
Entered: *also* Enter'd
Entre deux vins
Envergado: Honduran
Etched
Euaned: "[Prime Minister Tony] Blair has been more in touch with youth culture than previous prime ministers, showing himself to be a 'new dad' when his fifteen-year-old son Euan was found by the police lying drunk on a London street (leading to the latest playground word for drunk to be 'Euaned')." From Mike Storry and Peter Childs' *British Cultural Identities*.

EATIN' DIRT

Exalt: *also* Exalted

Excited: Cited by the *Lowell Daily Citizen and News* of September 9, 1856, as the latest slang for drunk: "We went out sober, and we came home 'excited.'"

Exhilarated

➤ EXTINGUISHED

Eyes like piss holes in the snow

[F]

Faced

Faceless (or *sans visage*)

Face walking

Faded

Faint

Fallen down: *also* Falling down drunk

Fap: From Shakespeare's *The Merry Wives of Windsor*, "The gentleman had drunk himself out of his five sentences...And being fap, sir, was, as they say, cashiered" (1598). The term appears in Noah Webster's 1806 *Dictionary* but is listed with the notation of *obs*.

Far ahead: *also* Farahead

Farmed

Farshnushked

Fearless: *also* Fears no man

Featured: Edmund Wilson says in a explanatory note to his 1927 "Lexicon of Prohbition" that this is a theatrical term which refers to a stage of drunkenness when "the social drinker is inspired to believe strongly in his ability to sing a song, to tell a funny story or to execute a dance..."

Fecked

Fed his kitty

EXTINGUISHED

Feelin' no pain
Feeling
Feeling aces
Feeling excellent
Feeling frisky
Feeling good: *also* Feeling pretty good; Feeling real well; Got the good feeling; Starting to feel pretty good; Sure feeling good
Feeling groovy
Feeling his alcohol
Feeling his booze
Feeling his cheerios
Feeling his drink: *also* Really feeling his drinks
Feeling his liquor: *also* Getting to feel his liquor
Feeling his oats: *also* Eating his oats; On his oats
Feeling his onions
Feeling it; *also* Feeling it a little
Feeling the effect
Fell off his budget
Feng schwasted: Defined by contributor Michael Donnelly in the Urban Dictionary as "a surrounding harmonious atmosphere encouraging of a state of intoxication: 'The girl in the kitchen with the pink skirt and holding a colorful bottle of vodka made Bob feel like getting *feng schwasted*.'"
Feng shuied
Fermented
Fetter'd
Fettled: *also* In good fettle
Feverish
Fiddle-cup
Fiddled
Fighting drunk

Fighting tight

Filled

Filled with courage: *also* Full of courage; Full of Dutch courage

Fired: *also* Fired up

➤ **FISH-EYED:** *also* Fishy-eyed

Fished

Fishy: *also* Fishey; Fishy about the gills

Fitzschnookered

Fixed: *also* Fixed up; In a fix; Well fixed

Fizzaded

Fizzed up

Fizzled

FISH EYED

Fizzy
Flabbergasted
Flag is out: *also* Has his flag out
Flag is outflanked
Flagged
Faint
Flaked out: *also* Flakers; Flako
Flambéd: *also* Flambayed
Flared

FLUFFY

Flatch kennurd

Flat-out drunk: *also* Flat-ass drunk

Flatten a sail

Flawed: *also* Flawd

Fleein'

Fleemered

Flickered

Floating: *also* Floatin'

Flooded: *also* Flooded his sewers

Flooey

Floopy

Floored

Floothered: from the West of Ireland

Floppy

Florid

Florious

Flostered

Flown with the wild turkey

➤ **FLUFFED:** *also* Fluffy

Flummoxed

Flurbed

Flush

Flushed: *also* A little flushed: "[Australian] Women do not
get drunk, or any of the many other lingoisms describing
that term, instead they get TIDDLY, or MERRY, or even more
politely, A LITTLE FLUSHED," according to *Lingo: Listening to
Australian English* by Graham Seal.

Flusterated

Flustered

Flusticated

Flustrated

Flutered: Defined in John Ash's *New and Complete Dictionary*

of the English Language (1795) as "half drunk" and used with
the word "with" as in "He was flutered with wine."

Fluthered

Fly-blown: *also* Flyblown: According to Farmer & Henley being "fly-blown" is a colonial term for being "done up."

Fly-by-night

Flying blind

Flying in the dirt

Flying light

Flying one wing low

Fnarkled

Fogged: *also* In a fog

Foggy: According to *The Slang Dictionary or The Vulgar Words,
Street Phrases and "Fast" Expressions of High and Low Society*
(London, 1884) "foggy" is a term for mild intoxication.

Fogmatic: In the 19th century, anti-fogmatic was a word for
raw rum or raw whiskey.

Folded

Foobed

Fool if you don't quit

Foolish

Footless

Foozlified

Fossilized

Fou: The term is widely regarded as especially common in
Scotland. "Wilbraham has *foudrunk*," i.e. is despicably drunk,
dead drunk. French, *fou*, mad, as *fouenragé*; or simply *fu, i.e.*
"full," "intensive," as in "*full-oft, full-well* ye reject the com-
mandment of God," according to *Brewer's Dictionary of Phrase
and Fable*, 1898.

Fou as a pugie

Fou as a wulk

Foul anchor

Four to the floor: Presumably a state in which one is on one's hands and knees, a play on the manual transmission of a sports car "four on the floor."

Foxed: *also* Fox'd; Foxt

Foxy

Fozzed

Fractured

Frayed

Frazzled

Freaked

Free

Freefall

Fresh: Listed in *The Slang Dictionary or The Vulgar Words, Street Phrases and "Fast" Expressions of High and Low Society* (London, 1884) as a term for mild intoxication.

Fresh way

Freshish

Fried: *also* Fried up; Half-fried: *The Dictionary of American Slang*, 1960 edition, completed the idiom of cuisine by adding "fried" to "boiled" and "stewed," meaning "intoxicated."

Fried on both sides

Fried to the gills

Fried to the hat

Front loaded: Specifically, getting drunk prior to an event where alcohol is not going to be served.

Frozen: *also* Almost froze; Almost frozen; Froze his mouth; Has froze his mouth

Fruit looped

FUBAR: Fucked Up Beyond All Recognition; also Fubar'd; Fubared

Fuck faced

Fucked: *also* All fucked up; Fucked out; Fucked over; Fucked up; All fucked up; Fuckered up

Fuddle: *also* Befuddled; Fuddled; Fuddling; In a fuddle; On the fuddle: The entry from John Ash's 1795 *New and Complete Dictionary of the English Language* notes: "To drink to excess; to get drunk." It also includes a separate entry as a transitive verb meaning "To intoxicate; to make drunk." This dictionary also lists *fuddlecap* for one who makes a practice of getting drunk.

Fueled

Full: *also* About full

Full-flavoured

Full as a boot

Full as a Bourke Street tram

Full as a bull

Full as a bull's bum

Full as a fairy's phone book

Full as a fart

Full as a fat woman's phone book

Full as a fiddler

Full as a flea: Phrase used by Rudyard Kipling in several novels and short stories.

Full as a footy final

Full as a goog: *also* Full as a goog egg: Defined in *Calibre*, a novel by Ken Bruen, 2006, as, "Extremely drunk. Comes from the Scottish word 'goggie,' a child's word for egg. It is a variation on an earlier Australian phrase in the same sense, 'full as a tick.' Later combinations include 'full as a Bourke Street tram' and 'full as a bull's bum.'"

Full as a goat

Full as a goose

Full as a lord

Full as a pig's ear

Full as a Pommy complaint-box: "Pommy" is Australian slang for a Brit; especially one who has recently immigrated.

Full as a pot: *also* Full as a po full; Full as the family po; Full as the family pot

Full as a seaside shithouse on bank holiday: *also* Full as a seaside shithouse on Boxing Day

Full as a state school

Full as a state school hatrack

Full as a tick

Full as a tick on a fat cow

Full as an egg

Full as the jerry: *also* Full as the family jerry

Full as two race trains

Full flavored

Full of loud mouth soup: In April, 2008, Tom Morton, a BBC correspondent based in the Shetland Islands, asked listeners to send terms for drunk to be woven into a poem. He got 26 winners which he used, but this was his favorite entry of all.

Full to the brim

Full up

Full up to the brain

Full-rigged

Fully kroizoned

Fung hoed

Funny: *also* Feeling funny

Fuzzle

Fup wasted

Fur brained

➤ **FUR ON HIS TONGUE**

➤ **FURRY**

Furschnickered

Fuzzled; *also* Fuzl'd
Fuzzy: *also* Fuzzy headed

[G]

Gaaaaaaaaaaa
Gaffed
Gaga

FUR ON HIS TONGUE

FURRY

Gaged: *also* Got the gage up; Has his gage up

Gaily

Gallows drunk

Galvanized

Gambrinous

Gansado: Portuguese

Ganted: Yorkshire, England

Gargled

Gashed

Gassed: *also* Gas'd; Gaseous; Gassed up; Really gassed

Gassosa: Italian

Gassy

Gatted

Gay

Gayed

Gazompt'd

Gazumped: Listed as current university slang by London's *Daily Mail*, in a December 8, 2000, article entitled "Student Speak? Most Parents Just Wouldn't Have A Scooby Doo."

Geared up: *also* All geared up; Half geared-up

Geed: *also* Geed up

Gee-eyed

Geesed

Geezed: *also* All geezed up; Geezed up

Generous

Geneva courage: The braggadocio which is the effect of having drunk too much gin. Gin is a corrupt contraction of "geneva," or, rather, of "*genièvre*."

Gestunketed

Get Chinese

Getting

Getting a loan on

Getting a thrill: *also* Got a thrill

Getting about all he needs

Getting absolutely Moulin Rouged

Getting an answer

Getting full: *also* Getting pretty full

Getting him

Getting his ears back

Getting in

Getting more nails for his coffin

Getting on the band wagon

Getting one on

Getting started: *also* Pretty well started

Getting the habit

Getting there

Getting to be a drunkard

Getting too full

Getting warmed: *also* Getting warmed up

Gibbled

Giddy

Giffed

Giggled

Giggly

Gild

Gilded

Gin crazed

Gin soaked

Gingered up

Ginned: *also* Ginned up; Ginned-up

Ginny

Gitted

Gizzled

Glad

Glassy

Glassy-eyed

Glazed: *also* Glaiz'd

Glazed like a $3 whore

Globular

Glorious: *also* Feeling glorious; Gloriously drunk: In an article entitled "The Gloriously Drunk Man" that appeared in *The Owl*, a British journal, January 23, 1884, he was defined as one who is "…usually ripe between one and three o'clock a.m., when, if he is not harvested by his friends and a hackman, he is liable to be pulled by the police."

Glowing: *also* Aglow; Beginning to get a glow on; Getting a glow; Glowed; Got a glow on; Had a glow on; Has a glow on; Has a pretty good glow on; In a glow; Starting to glow

Glued

Goat drunk

God-awful drunk

Goggled

Goggle-eyed

Going

Going overboard

Going to Jerusalem

Gold-headed

Golfed

Gone: *also* A little gone; About gone; All gone; Completely gone; Far gone; Five winos gone; Half-gone; Pretty far gone; Quite gone; Three parts gone; Well gone

Gone Borneo

Gone Canadian

Gone down in flames

Gone maximum Southern Comfort

Gone out: *also* Goes out

Gone over the Cognac Trail

Gone over the hill

➤ **GONE TO THE DEVIL**

Gonged

Gonzo

Goo goo eyed

Gooched

Good and drunk

Good to go

GONE TO THE DEVIL

Goofied

Goofy: *also* Getting goofy

Googly

Googled

Googly-eyed

Gooned

Goosed

Gorillas: *also* Gorillas in the mist: Contemporary UK rhyming slang, from the film *Gorillas In The Mist*, for "pissed." Listed as new slang in "Can you Speak da lingo8? OUR A-Z GUIDE TO THE ENGLISH LANGUAGE TODAY" in *The People* (London, England, Jan 13, 2008).

Gory-eyed

Got a blow on

Got a crumb in his beard

Got a dish

Got a little Polly on

Got a rum nose

Got a skate on: *also* Has a skate on; On a skate; With a skate on

Got barley fever

Got by the head

Got Corns in his Head

Got glass eyes

Got his beer on board

Got his nose wet: This entry comes courtesy of Don Crinklaw in a letter to the author, dated December 29, 1981, explaining, "I've only heard one person use it, my grandmother, and it was in the 1940s, and it had to do with my grandfather stopping at a tavern for a few beers before he came home. Since Grandpa never got spifflicated, schnoggered, blitzed or any of those things, Grandma used it only to mean stopping at, etc., and not getting bollixed, fried or fizzled. But it sure sounds like it *could* mean all those things. And as I remember, Grandma disapproved."

Got his shoes full

➤ **GOT HIS SNOWSUIT ON AND HEADING NORTH**

Got kibbled heels

Got more than he can carry

➤ **GOT MY BEER GOGGLES ON**

Got on his little hat: *also* Has got his little hat on

Got one going

Got some in him

Got the flavour: *also* Has got the flavor

Got the glanders

Got the gout

GOT HIS SNOWSUIT ON
AND HEADING NORTH

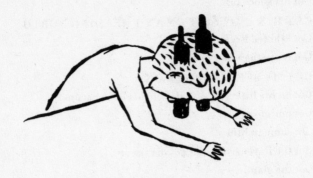

GOT MY BEER GOGGLES ON

Got the gravel rash: This term appears in *The Slang Dictionary or The Vulgar Words, Street Phrases and "Fast" Expressions of High and Low Society* (London, 1884) as a term for the highest level of intoxication.

Got the Indian vapors

Got the nightmare

Got the Pole Evil

Got the treatment

Got too much: *also* Had a little too much

Got up to the third story

Got warmed

Got whizzy: *also* Getting a little whizzy

Gouged

Gowed: *also* All gowed up; Gowed to the gills; Gowed up

Grade-A Certified Drunk

Grapeshot: *also* Grape-shot

Grass grabbin'

Graved

Gravelled

Greased: *also* Well greased

Greetin' fu'

Groatable

Grog: *Blackguardiana*, 1794, lists "grog" as: "groggy, drunk."

Grogged: *also* Grogged up; On the grog

Groggy

Guarding the Gates of Hell

Gubbed

Gubbered

Gunned

Gurning: Probably inspired by the British slang verb "to gurn," which means to pull grotesque faces.

Gut fucked

Guts up

Gutted

Gutter drunk: *also* Gutter sleepin' drunk; In the gutter

Guttered

Guyed out: *also* All guyed up

Guzzled: *Blackguardiana*, 1794, lists "guzzle" as a noun for liquor.

[H]

Haaaaaaaaaaa

Habuji

Had a couple of drinks

Had a couple of shooters

Had a dram

Had a few drinks

Had a few too many

Had a little

Had a little too many

Had a number of beers

Had a shot or two

Had a snort

Had a toothful

Had enough: *also* Got about enough

Had enough to make him noisy

Had his cold tea

Had it: *also* About had it; 'Bout had it

Had one or two

Had tutu (two too) many

Haily gaily

Hair on his tongue

Half and half

Half drunk: Pitcher David Wells claimed in a book that he was "half drunk" when he pitched a perfect game for the New York Yankees on May 17, 1998. And there is this usage, from a 19th-century American ballad:

> HARD TIMES:
> *Next is the tinker, he'll mend all your ware,*
> *For little or nothing, some ale or some beer;*
> *But before he begins, he'll get half drunk or more,*
> *And in stopping one hole, why he'll punch twenty more.*

Half in the boot

Half jigged

Half kicked in the ass: *also* Two-thirds kicked in the ass

➤ **HALF NELSON**

Half seas over: *also* Half-sea; Half-seas under: Defined in *Brewer's Dictionary of Phrase and Fable*, 1898, as "Now applied

to a person almost *dead* drunk. The phrase seems to be a corruption of the Dutch *op-zee zober*, 'over-sea beer,' a strong,
heady beverage introduced into Holland from England."

Half-assed

Half-bulled

Half-rinsed

Half-sober

Half-stoused

Halfway over

Halfway to Baghdad

Halfway to Concord

Hammer-blowed

Hammered: When a new vodka brand "Thor's Hammer" was
announced in 2000, those marketing the product insisted
that the name refered to the Norse god of thunder and his

HALF NELSON

hammer, which returned to him boomerang-style after he hurled it at enemies. The marketing folks insisted that that name had no connection with the word "hammered," slang for getting really drunk. The brand was pitched at male consumers between the ages of 25 and 35.

Hammerish

Hammied

Hamstered

Hanced

Hang a gem on

Hang one on

Hanging

Happy: *also* Feeling happy; Happy drunk; Pretty happy; Quite happy; Slappin' happy; Unco' happy

Hard

Hard up: *also* Hard-up

Hardwankered

Hardy

Harping it home

Harry flakers

Has a big head: *also* Got the big head

Has a brass eye: *also* Got a brass eye: In his *Drinker's Dictionary* Benjamin Franklin lists this term but it is also cited by Walter Machos in *The New York Times*, December 2, 1956, as a recent coinage. The origin of this coinage is unknown but in modern slang "brass eye" is slang for the anus. It was also the name for a BBC series of mockumentaries.

Has a can on

Has a drop too much taken

Has a perma smile

Has a rubber drink: Listed by Edmund Wilson in his "Lexicon of Prohibition." This may refer to the concept of "bounce" as with a "rubber check."

Has a sausage: The *Washington Post*, February 22, 1903, reported this as a term for drunk in New Orleans.

Has a skinful: *also* Had a skinful and a half

Has a slant on: *also* With a slant on

Has a turkey on one's back: *also* Got a turkey on one's back: One of the terms for being drunk popular during the War Between the States according to John D. Wright's *The Language of the Civil War*. The cumbersome turkey is something one had on one's back when one was drunk—analogous, perhaps, to "he's got a monkey on his back" for drug addiction.

Has been paid

Has burnt his Shoulder: *also* He's burnt his Shoulder

Has business on

Has dampened his mug

Has diluted the blood in his alcohol system

Has drank more than he has bled

Has gallon distemper

Has had a Thump over the Head with Sampson's Jawbone

Has his head full of bees

Has his head on backwards

Has his malt above his wheat

Has hung one on

Has lost a shoe

Has made an example

Has Made Too Free With John Barleycorn: *also* A date with John Barleycorn; Loaded with John Barleycorn: Barleycorn is the long-established personification of beer, whiskey, and other intoxicating drinks made from malted barley. Dating to at least 1620, it owes its popularity to Robert Burns, who used the expression freely throughout the body of his poetry. In the poem "John Barleycorn," Burns uses the processing of the grain to produce whiskey as a symbol of man's life, death, and rebirth. The personified "john barleycorn" is reaped, ground, roasted, and distilled; his life's blood is drunk by the men of Scotland bringing them happiness and boldness; finally:

> *But the cheerful spring came kindly on*
> *And show'rs began to fall;*
> *John Barleycorn got up again,*
> *And sore surprised them all.*

Has scalt his head pad

Has seen the yellow star

Has stole a manchet out of the brewer's basket

Has swallow'd a tavern token

Has taken a chiruping glass

Has taken Hippocrates' grand elixir

Has the blue Johnnies

Has the Indian vapors

Has the Mexican vapors

Has the rats: *also* Half rats; Half-rats; In the rats

Has the screaming meemies

Has the shakes

Has the uglies

Has the whoops and jingles

Has the yorks

Has the zings

Has yellow fever

Hat rack

Haunted with Evil Spirits

Have a tumble down the sink

Having a close look at the footpath

Having a cooler

Having a warmer

Having the eyes opened

Having the whirlygigs

Haywire

Hazy: Listed in *The Slang Dictionary or The Vulgar Words, Street Phrases and "Fast" Expressions of High and Low Society* (London, 1884) as a term for mild intoxication.

He bet on the wrong bottle

He couldn't find his ass with two hands

He couldn't find his behind with a big mirror in broad daylight

He couldn't find his behind with a search warrant

He couldn't scratch his rear with buckhorns

He cuts his capers

He drank so much hair-oil he had to eat moth balls to keep down the fur

He drank till he gave up his Half-Penny

He had a full-growed case of booze blind

He has looked on the sun when it was red

He makes Virginia fence: Found in Benjamin Franklin's *The Drinker's Dictionary* (1737). And explained in *A 19th Century Slang Dictionary* by Craig Hadley as, "A staggering drunk was said to make this (a zigzagging fence) when he walked. Anyone or anything that meanders. Any fence constructed in this manner."

He never knowed he had a twin brother 'til he looked in the mirror behind the bar

He sees the bears

He took his drops

He's contending with Pharaoh

He's eat the Cocoa Nut

He's eat a toad and a half for breakfast

He's heat his copper

He's kiss'd black Betty: "Betty," according to Louise Pound writing in *American Speech*, was an early term for "spirit bottle," appearing as early as 1725.

He's Prince Eugene

He's right before the wind with all his studding sails out

Heading into the wind

Heady

Hear the owl hoot

Hearty

Heated

Heavy drunk

Hebriated

Heckled

Hee-hawing around

Heeled

Heeled over

Heinous

Helmutschmitted: This is clearly an eponymous use of the name Helmut Schmidt, former German finance minister and chancellor who was 90 when this book went to press. But why? Not known as an excessive drinker, he is a chain cigarette smoker who commonly lights up during interviews, giving the impression of man who cannot control his vice even on camera.

Helpless

Hepped: *also* Hepped up

Heroic

Het-up

Hiccins: From "To Express the Condition of 45 on a Merry Pin," *New London Gazette*, December 13, 1771, which notes "probably from hiccuping."

Hiccius-doccius: *also* Hicksius doxius

Hickey

Hickory-smoked

Hiddey

High: *also* Been flying rather high; Feeling high; Floating high; Flying high; Getting a little high; Getting kind of high; Getting pretty high; Getting up high; Half-high; Kind of high; Pretty high; Rather high; Really high; Slightly high; Very high

High as a cat's back at a dog show

High as a fiddler's fist

High as a Georgia pine

High as a giraffe's balls

High as a kite: *also* Higher than a kite

High as Lindbergh

High as steam off a cold cow turd

High as the price of gold

High as the sky

High behind

High in the saddle

High lonesome

High up to picking cotton

Hipped

His breath was near strong 'nough to crack a mirror

His elevator's stalled

His hair hurts

HIS HEAD IS SMOKING

His lee scuppers are under

His nose is red: *also* His nose is getting red

His Shoe pinches him

His teeth are floating

Hit and missed: Cockney rhyming slang for "pissed"

Hit by a barnmouse: *also* Been hit by a barn mouse; bitten by a barn-mouse

Hit on the head by a tavern bitch

Hitting 'em up

HIS HEAD IS SMOKING

Hitting it a little

Hitting the jug

Hitting the ruby

Hoary-eyed

Hockey: *also* Hocky

Hocus: According to *Blackguardiana*, 1794, to be quite "hocus" is to be quite drunk.

Hocus-pocus

Hog drunk: *also* Drunk as a hog

Hog whimpering: *also* Hog-whimpering drunk: Writing in *The Guardian* on March 6, 1996, Simon Hoggart suggests that this term was once used by the upper class for one who is extremely and incoherently drunk.

Hog wild

Hoisting the elegant

Holding up the wall

Honked

Hooched: *also* Hooched up

Hoodman

Hooked by a fat one

Hooshed

Hooted

Hopped: *also* Hopped up

Horizontal

Horizontal Horseback

Hornson: *also* Got the horns on; Got the Hornson

Hosed

Hot: This term was found in "Drunk," a list in the *Weekly Eagle* of Brattleboro, Vermont, in 1851. It still seems to have currency. In an article in *Yankee* magazine of March, 1995, a man living in Northern Vermont tells of going into the Air Force and hearing "hot" as a word applied exclusively to women: "Where we came from 'get hot' meant 'get drunk.'"

Hot as a red wagon

Hot headed

Hotsy-totsy

Hotter than a skunk

Housed

How came ye so?: *also* How-came-you-so?; How-come-ye-so?

How fare ye

Howling

Humidified

Hummin'

Hung up proper
Humored: *also* Good-humored
Hurt
Hurting a turtle

[I]

Iaaaaaaaaaaaaaaaaa
Iced: *also* Half-iced
Iced to the eyebrows
Illuminated
"I'm not as think as you drunk I am."
Imbibed
Imbibed giggle water
Imbibed too freely
Impaired
Impixocated
In a bad way
In a delicate condition
In a difficulty
In a ditch
In a drunken stupor
In a head
In a trance
In a vise
➡ **IN ARMOR:** *also* In his armor; In one's armour
In bed with one's boots on: meaning extremely intoxicated;
passed out. The reference is, of course, to one so inebriated
that he cannot take his boots off before going to bed.
In color
In drink: *also* Down in drink: Nell Gwynn was a sometime bawd
and actresss who became one of Charles II's mistresses. Nell's

IN ARMOR

mother, who was a working prostitute all her life, fell into a ditch and drowned. It was recorded that, "She had been 'in drink' at the time of her accident."

In for it: *also* Well in for it

In high glee: In an 1803 assesment of the condition of weekend revelers (*From Weekly Visitor or Ladies' Miscellany*, June 18, 1803), this is a condition between sober and "drunkish," followed by "staggering," "tipsy," "muzzy" and "dead drunk"—hence a milder form of inebriation.

In his airs

In his ales

In his beer

In his elements

In his glory

In his habits

In his prosperity

In it now

In liquor: Found in Benjamin Franklin's "The Drinker's Dictionary." And John Russell Bartlett in his *Dictionary Of Americanisms* of 1848 lists this as an Americanism.

In Liquor-Pond Street: *also* In liquor-pond: An actual street in London housing brewers and distillers. From the records of the Old Bailey, January 15, 1692: "Anne Brodnix was tried for being accessory to James and Abraham Stacy in the Felony and Robbery they lately committed in the House of William Kent a Brewer in Liquor-Pond Street ..."

In one's altitudes: *also* In his altitudes; Out of altitudes

In one's cups: *also* In his cups; In your cups

In orbit: *also* In his orbit

In tatters

In the blues

In the cellar

In the clouds

In the grip of the grape

In the gun: Defined in *Blackguardiana*, 1794, as "GUN, he's in the gun, he is drunk, perhaps from an allusion to a vessel called a gun, used for ale in the universities."

In the ozone

In the pen

In the pink

In the pulpit

In the satchel

In the suds: *also* A little in the suds; In the Sudds; Into the suds

In the sun: *also* Been in the sun; Standing too long in the sun

In the tank: *also* Half in the tank

In the wind

In the wrapper: *also* Half in the wrapper

In uncharted waters

Incog

Incognitibus

Incognito

Indentured

Indisposed

Inebriate

Inebriated: *also* Getting a little inebriated; Getting inebriated

Infirm

Inflaminated

Influenced

Injun drunk

Inked

Inkypoo

Insobriety

Inspired
Inter pocula
Into it: *also* Well into it
Intoxed
Intoxicate
Intoxicated: *also* Almost intoxicated; Getting intoxicated; Pleasantly intoxicated; Pretty well intoxicated; Thoroughly intoxicated: The earliest use for this term is in the proceedings of the Old Bailey, January 15, 1703, in which a man is given a "Pint of Brandy, which intoxicated him."
Inundated
Invigorated
Invincible
Invisible
Invisi-blind
Irish: *also* Feeling Irish
Ironed-out
Iron-plated
Irrigated
Irrigated the ulcers
Ishkimmisk
It's beginning to kick
It's getting to him
It's got ahold of him and he can't let go
It's working on him

[J]

Jaaaaaaaaaaaaaaaaaaaa
Jackassed: *also* Jack assed
Jacked
Jaegered

Jag: *also* A jag on; Getting a jag on; Got a jag on; Has a full jag on; Has a jag on; Jag on; Jag up; Jagg'd; Jagged; Jagged up; On a jag; With a jag on: Seen as a euphemistic Americanism when it was argued that the word "drunk" only "applied to tramps." The *Boston Globe* of May 24, 1910, wrote, "The word 'jag' is American slang for intoxication. Originally, 'jag' meant a small load, and when load grew to be a synonym for 'drunk,' 'jag' was humorously substituted for a small drunk. But it is now applied to the most imposing form of intoxication." And an article in the *Daily Inter Ocean* (Chicago) for May 20, 1889, entitled "A Serpent with a Jag on," tells of a black snake which consumes more than a quart of corn liquor from a general store. It returns a day later, is allowed to drink its fill and is then killed.

Jahalered

Jaked: *also* Jaiked up

Jambled

Jammed: According to an article in the April 23, 1922, *New York Times* entitled "'Argo' of the Shifters," this was flapper slang for drunk and appears in a glossary along with "cat's pajamas" used to describe "anything very good."

Jan Michael Vincented

Jan'd: Abbreviation for Jan Michael Vincented

Jarred

Jaxied

Jazzed: *also* Jazzed up

Jd'd to the max

Jickey

Jiggered

Jim-jams: *also* Has the jim jams

Jimmy Hendrixed

Jingled: *also* Pleasantly jingled: A term preferred by Jack London in his book on drinking, *John Barleycorn: Mr. London's*

Graphic Story Of Personal Experiences. The August 24, 1913, *New York Times* review of the book by poet Joyce Kilmer notes that London is inexplicably unable to come up with more than this one synonym for drunk. Edmund Wilson in his 1927 hierarchy of terms for drunk lists it as the seventh mildest form of the condition after "lit," "squiffy," "oiled," "lubricated," "owled," and "edged."

Jober as a sudge: This is a spoonerism for "Sober as a Judge" and an excuse for hauling out this old exchange:

> Defendant: I was drunk as a judge when I committed the offense.
>
> Judge: The expression is "sober as a judge." Don't you mean "drunk as a lord"?
>
> Defendant: Yes, my lord.

Jocular

Joe b'd

John Bull: Australian (not Cockney) rhyming slang for "full." According to Antonio Lillo, it has been used since the 1960s.

Jolly

Jolly fu'

Joplined

Joused

Jovial: From New York café owner Roland Elliot's 1913 collection, term for being mildly drunk.

Joyous

Jubilated: According to an article in the *Morning Oregonian*, June 28, 1897, this was a term applied to those celebrating excessively in London at the time of Queen Victoria's Golden Jubilee, which was celebrated on the 20th and 21st of June, 1887. It is a blend of "Jubilee" and "Intoxicated."

Jug-bitten

Jug up a fair one

Jugged: *also* Jugged up

Jug-steamed

Juiced: *also* Feeling juiced up; Juiced up; On the juice

Juice-looped

Juicy

Jumbo's trunk: Cockney rhyming slang for "drunk."

Jungled

Just south of bejesus

[K]

Kaaaaaaaaaaaaa

Ka-floot

Kaiboshed

Kalidekeemooed

Kalied: Term from the British television series of the mid-1990s, *Coronation Street*, which was also in large part responsible for the Briticism "cheeky monkey." (See "Coronation Speak" in the *Daily Mirror*, September 10, 1996.)

Kaned

Kaylide up

Kaylide: *Oxford English Dictionary* lists as "origin unknown"; the earliest reference given is in the 1937 edition of *Partridge's Dictionary of Slang* where it is noted as from circa 1927.

Keel-hauled

Keg-legged

Kennedied

Kennurd: George H. McKnight wrote in his 1923 work *English Words and Their Background* that this word was a by-product of World War I during which "…the co-mingling of social classes brought to the surface a rich variety of words belonging to the speech of submerged classes in Great Brit-

ain, words exhibiting the form of humor everywhere charac-
teristic of slang. Words of this class which have been recently
cited are: 'daisy roots,' 'boots;' 'almond rocks,' 'socks;' 'artful dodger,' 'lodger;' 'isabeller,' 'umbrella;' 'field of wheat,'
'street;' 'cherry ripe,' 'pipe;' 'suppose,' 'nose,' etc. In this
underworld speech a popular method of word formation is
back slang, or *Kacab genals*, consisting of words with letters
inverted from the normal, as in *elrig*, 'girl'; *Kennurd*, 'drunk';
yennep, 'penny.'"

Kentucky-fried

Kershnickered

Kettled: This has the whiff of antiquity attached to it, but it
was also listed as current university slang by London's *Daily
Mail*, on December 8, 2000, in an article entitled "Student
Speak? Most Parents Just Wouldn't Have A Scooby Doo."

Keyed: *also* Keyed up

Keyed to the roof

Kicked in the guts: Had a kick in the guts; Has been kicked in
the guts; Has had a kick in the guts

Killed

Killed his dog

Kippered

Kisk: *also* Kisky: This term appears in *The Slang Dictionary or
The Vulgar Words, Street Phrases and "Fast" Expressions of High
and Low Society* (London, 1884) as a term for mild intoxication.

Kited

Knackered

Knapt

**Knee-crawling, commode-hugging, gutter-wallowing
drunk**

Knee-walkin': *also* Knee-walking drunk

Knocked for a loop: *also* Knocked to a loop

Knocked off his pins
Knocked out
Knocked over
Knocked South
Knocked-up
Knockered
Knows not the way home
Knus-drunk
 KO'D

KO'D

Kraeusened

Kursasted

Ky-eyed

[L]

La femme drunkita

Laaaaaaaaaaaaaaaaaaaaaaaaaaa

Laced

Lagered

Lagged up

Laid: *also* Laid out; Laid right out

Laid to the bone

Lame

Lamped

Langerated

Langered: *also* Langers: "Where does this come from?" asked
Victoria Moore in her June 17, 2002, article on terms for
drunk in the *New Statesman*. "Well, apparently, langer also
means penis—probably a corruption of 'long one'—so we're
back to boys'-night-out vocabulary again."

Lapped

Lapped the gutter: *also* Lap in the gutter; Lap the gutter: This
term appears in *The Slang Dictionary or The Vulgar Words, Street
Phrases and "Fast" Expressions of High and Low Society* (London,
1884) as a term for the highest level of intoxication.

Lappy

Lappy legged

Laroped

Larruped: *also* Larrupt

Larruping drunk

Lashed

Lathered: *also* Lathered up; Well lathered

Laughing at the carpet

Lazarus: *also* Keilazarus: Dutch

Leaked

Leaning: *also* Leanin'

Leaping: *also* Leaping up

Leathered

Leery: *also* Leary

Legless: *also* Leg-less: So drunk one is unable to walk. It would appear to be of recent origin. *Oxford Engish Dictionary* lists 1976 as the earliest use, in a song title: "Wide eyed and legless."

Less than vital

Letting the finger ride the thumb

Leveled

Licked (as in liquored up)

Lifted

Lifting the little finger

Liggidy-loaded

Light

Light on top

Light-headed: *also* Getting light-headed

Lighting up

Lights out

Like a Rat in Trouble

Like Christmas

Likkered: *also* Getting likkered up; Likkered up

Likkerous

Likker-soaked

Lillian Gished: "Pished" as in "pissed," Cockney rhyming slang, courtesy of Antonio Lillo.

Limber

Limp

Limp-legged

Lined

Lion drunk

Liquefied

Liquidated

Liquor plug

Liquor struck

Liquored: *also* Liquored up; All liquored up

Liquorish

Liquor's talking

Listened to the owl hoot

Listing to starboard

Lit: *also* A bit lit; Bit lit; Getting lit; Getting pretty well lit; Half-lit; Lit a bit; So lit you could read by him; Really lit; Well lit: Found in Edmund Wilson's 1927 list of synonyms based on "degrees of intensity," "lit" is the mildest, followed by "squiffy," "oiled," "lubricated," "owled," "edged," "jingled," "piffed," "piped," and "sloppy." One of the odder etymologies for this term was sent to me by someone in the UK: "It so happens that those who drink quantities of liquor generally end up with a red nose. This in slang, is a 'lantern' or 'lighthouse.' It's quite obvious that such a 'lantern' is 'lit' by imbibing more liquor."

Lit to the gills

Lit to the guards

Lit to the gunnels

Lit up: *also* All lit up; Getting lit up; Lit up a little bit; Really lit up; Starting to get lit up

Lit up like a ballroom

Lit up like a carnival ride

Lit up like a cathedral

Lit up like a Chanukah bush

Lit up like a Christmas tree

Lit up like a church

Lit up like a firefly

Lit up like a honky-tonk on a Saturday night

Lit up like a kite

Lit up like a lantern

Lit up like a lighthouse

Lit up like a skyscraper

Lit up like a store window

Lit up like Broadway

Lit up like high mass

Lit up like London

Lit up like Main Street

Lit up like the Commonwealth

Lit up like the sky

Lit up like the Star of Bethlehem

Lit up like Times Square

Lit up to show he's human

Little off the beam

Little round the corner

Liver-lubed

Living up a bit

➤ **LIZA MINELLIED**

Loaded: *also* Fully loaded; Getting loaded; Getting his load on;
Got a load on; Has a full load on; Has a load on; Has a load under
the skin; Really got a load; Really had a load; Well loaded; With
a load on: The term appears in an article about new youth slang
in the *Brooklyn Eagle* of June 19,1925, "Such Slanguage Nowadys
Parents Require Lexicon To Interpret Offspring."

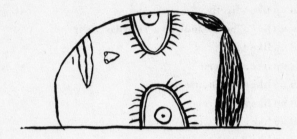

LIZA MINELLIED

Loaded for bear
Loaded his cart
Loaded to the barrel
Loaded to the earlobes
Loaded to the eyebrows
Loaded to the gills
Loaded to the guards
Loaded to the gunnels
Loaded to the gunwales
Loaded to the hat
Loaded to the muzzle

Loaded to the plimsoll mark
Loaded to the tailgate
Loaded up on grapes
Loaded with bootleg
Loaded with firewater
Loaded with John Hall
Loading up
Locked
Locked out of your mind: Irish
Lock-legged
Locoed: *also* Locoed out
Locoed out on an 8-ball
Logged
Long Island tea'd
Longlong: Pidgin English
Longwhiskey: Pidgin English
Loo la
Looking like "weekend at Bernie's"
Looking lively: *also* Look lively
Looking through a glass
Loony
Loop-legged: *also* Looped-legged; Loopy-legged
Looped: *also* Getting looped; Half-looped; Slightly looped
Looping
Loopy
Loose: *also* Getting loose; On the loose
Loose in the hilt(s)
Loosening up
Lop-eared
Loppy
Lordly
Lordy

➤ LOST HIS BOOTS
Lost his rudder: *also* Somebody stole his rudder
Loud and proud
Lousy drunk
Low in the saddle
Lubed: *also* Lubed up
Lubricated: *also* Well lubricated
Lukewarm: From New York café owner Roland Elliot's 1913
collection, term for being mildly drunk.

Lumped

Lumpy: Defined in *The Slang Dictionary or The Vulgar Words, Street Phrases and "Fast" Expressions of High and Low Society* (London, 1884) as a term for a more intense state of beastliness that comes beyond mild intoxication and before total fuddlement.

Lush: *also* In lush; Lushed, Lushed up, Lushed-up

Lushington

Lushy

Lutoned: Allusion to the free drinks policy at London's Luton airport as advertised on its website: "Business and leisure travellers alike are assured a warm welcome from the friendly staff at the Aviance Airport lounge at Luton. Relax and watch the TV, listen to music or simply enjoy the quiet and calm whilst you are served free drinks before your flight."

[M]

Macked

Mad with it: *also* Mad wey it

Maggoted

Maggoty

Magoogled

Main-brace well spliced: *also* With the mainbrace well spliced

Making a trip to Baltimore

Making fun

Making indentures with one's legs

Making m's and i's

Malted

Mandoo-ed

Mangled

Manky

Mareado: Spanish which has found its way into the language of US bars.

Marinated

Martin-drunk: According to *Brewer's Dictionary of Phrase and Fable,* 1898, the term means, "Very intoxicated indeed; a drunken man 'sobered' by drinking more. The feast of St. Martin (November 11) used to be held as a day of great debauch. Hence Baxter uses the word 'Martin' as a synonym of a drunkard."

Mary Queen of Scots

Mashed

Massacred

Mastok

Materially altered: Fasionable euphemism for the condition of "votary of Bacchus" in the June 4, 1859, issue of *Punch.*

Maudle: The term is listed in John Ash's 1795 *New and Complete Dictionary of the English Language* as a verb meaning "to put out of order, to besot, to make half drunk." Derived from "the picture of Mary Maudlin."

Maudlin: *also* Trifle maudlin: "Stupidly sentimental. 'Maudlin drunk' is the drunkenness which is sentimental and inclined to tears. 'Maudlin slip-slop' is sentimental chitchat. The word is derived from Mary Magdalen, who is drawn by ancient painters with a lackadaisical face, and eyes swollen with weeping," this according to *Brewer's Dictionary of Phrase and Fable,*1898.

Maudling: Appears in John Ash's 1795 *New and Complete Dictionary of the English Language* as, "Getting half drunk, disordering with drink; drunken, fuddled."

Mauled: James Caulfield's *Blackguardiana* defines the term as "extremely drunk, or soundly beaten."

Mawbrish

Mawlin: According to the entry for this word in John Ash's 1795 *Dictionary*, it is a variant spelling of 'maudlin.'

Maxed: *also* Maxed out

Mean

Medicinally drunk: Particular state induced by alcohol prescribed for medical use. A Lieutenant Dunbar of the Royal Marines was acquitted of the charge of ungentlemanly conduct based on being overprescribed (*The Satirist; or, the Censor of the Times*, December 7, 1845).

Mealy mouthed

Meff'd

Mellifluous

Mega-drunk

Mellow: *also* Mellowing; Mellowish; Real mellow: In Langston Hughes's 1958 "How Many Words for 'Drunk?'" "mellow" is what his fictional informant on the language of the streets, known simply as Simple, says is the term for the "least drunk …when you have just a slight buzz on…" It is followed by "tipsy", "lubricated" and "high." Although this term seems modern, it is also listed in Franklin's "The Drinker's Dictionary" (1737). Samuel Johnson's *Dictionary of the English Language, Second Edition*, 1755-6, lists as his fourth meaning of this term "Drunk; melted down with drink."

Miraculous

Melted

Merle Haggard

Merloaded

Merry

Merry as a Greek

Mesmerized

Messed: *also* Messed up; Out messing up

Methodistconated: A Prohibition construct.

Mexican-fried

Mickey Monk: According to research into Irish rhyming slang by Antonio Lillo, the term is not "Mickey monked," but "Mickey Monk," rhyming with "drunk." Dr. Lillo also notes this term is exclusively Irish. Therefore it would be wrong to say that it is "Cockney" rhyming slang.

Mickey-finished

Middling: *also* Middlin'

Miffy

Milled

Minced

Ming mong: Falkirk, Scotland

Ming-ho

Minging: *also* Mingin': Scotland

Miraculous

Mitered

Mixed: *also* Mixed up

Mizzled: The *Oxford English Dictionary* entry note on the first usage gives the date of 1840, and the quote: "I've been thinking of lowering the quarter boat down, when they are a little more mizzled.... Frenchmen haven't the heads for drinking that Englishmen have."

Moccasined: Obsolete U.S. slang for drunk first cited in J. R. Bartlett's *Dictionary of Americanisms* in 1859. In the South a man made drunk by bad liquor is said to have been 'bitten by the [moccasin] snake,' or simply to be moccasined.

Mog-galore

Moired

Moist around the edges

Moistened

Mokus

Mollared up

Mollo

Molly

Monged

Monkey assed

Monkey-full

Monstered

Moon-eyed

Moonlit

Moonshined

Moony: *also* Mooney: Listed in *The Slang Dictionary or The Vulgar Words, Street Phrases and "Fast" Expressions of High and Low Society* (London, 1884) as a term for mild intoxication.

Mopped

Moppy

Mops and brooms: *also* All mops and brooms: A British usage, back to the early 19th century. The early context suggests it alludes to being on the floor "down with the mops and brooms." Thomas Hardy's use of the expression in *Tess of the d'Urbervilles* (1891) makes its meaning clear: "there is not much doing now, being New Year's Eve, and folks mops and brooms from what's inside 'em."

According to the glossary appended to George MacDonald Fraser's *Black Ajax*, to be "on the mop" is to be on a drinking spree.

More drunk than words can say

More or less in liquor

Mortal

Mortal drunk: *also* Mortally drunk: Newcastle, England

Mortaled

Mortallious

Mothered

Motherless

Mottled

Mountous

Mouthy

Moved

Mowed over

Muckibus

Muddled: *also* In a muddle; Muddled up; On the muddle:
According to Noah Webster's definition: "Made turbid; half
drunk; stupified."

Muddy

Muffed

Mug blots

Mugged: *also* Mugged up

Muggy: Listed in *The Slang Dictionary or The Vulgar Words,
Street Phrases and "Fast" Expressions of High and Low Society*
(London, 1884) as a term for mild intoxication.

Mulakered

Mulled: *also* Mulled up

Mullered: This is modern British university slang listed by
London's *Daily Mail*, on December 8. 2000, in an article entitled "Student Speak? Most Parents Just Wouldn't Have A Scooby
Doo." It is also listed in the *Lonely Planet British Phrasebook* for
the overseas visitor, which has been produced with the aim of
explaining English as it is really spoken, with no fewer than 64
additional words to describe alcoholic indulgence.

Mullet-eyed

Mullocked

Mummified: From New York café owner Roland Elliot's 1913 collection, term for completely drunk.

Munted: Defined in the online Kiwi-English Dictionary by a Wellington, NZ, man whose *nom d'net* is Brooksie: "Uum, 'not working as intended,' i.e., shit-faced, wasted, drunk off your arse. You get the picture! Have also heard this describe things as well, as in, 'That car's munted, it's not going anywhere!' Yes! Yet another synonym for 'drunk,' and a particularly good one, I might add."

Muntered: Contemporary university slang for drunk, according to London's *Daily Mail*, in a December 8, 2000, article entitled "Student Speak? Most Parents Just Wouldn't Have A Scooby Doo."

Muntit

Mushy

Muttonised (off me chops)

Muzzed

Muzzy: *also* Muzzey: In an 1803 assessment of weekend revelers this is a condition between sober and "drunkish," followed by "staggering," "tipsy," "muzzy" and "dead drunk"—hence a milder form of inebriation, from *Weekly Visitor or Ladies' Miscellany*, June 18, 1803.

[N]

Nailed to the floor

Nappy: *Blackguardiana*, 1794, lists as a cant term for "strong ale."

Nase

Nasty drunk

Native (as in "he went native")

N'awlins'ed up

Nazy: *also* Nazie

Nazzy: Given as a cant word for drunk in *The Triumph Of Wit: Or, The Canting Dictionary. Being The Newest And Most Useful Academy:....Illustrated With Poems, Songs, And Various Intrigues In The Canting Language, With The Explanation, &C.* Dublin, [1780?]. A "nazzy cove" in this volume is a drunkard.

Nearly off his rocker

Needing a reef taken in

Neoned

Newcastled

Newted

Nice

Nicely boxed

Nicely irrigated with horizontal lubricant

Nimptopsical

Nipped

Nished

Nissed as a pewt

Nodded

Noddy-headed

Noggy: *also* Nogy

Nolo

Non compos mentis: *also* Non compos

Non compos poopoo

Non se ipse

Noodled

Not all there

Not feeling any pain: *also* Feeling no pain; Hasn't got no pain; Not in any pain; Not suffering any; Suffering no pain

Not in Kansas anymore

Not so far from puken

Not-suckin

Nuked
Numb: *also* Comfortably numb
➤ **NUTS**
Nutty

NUTS

[O]

Oaaaaaaaaaa

➤ **OARED**

OARED

Obfuscated: Defined in *The Slang Dictionary or The Vulgar Words, Street Phrases and "Fast" Expressions of High and Low Society* (London, 1884) as a term for a more intense state of beastliness that comes beyond mild intoxication and before total fuddlement.

Obfusticated

Obliterated

Oblonctorated

Obnoxicated: A combination of "intoxicated" and "obnoxious" coined by Louis Jordan in his 1947 hit song, "Open the Door, Richard."

Oenophlygia: Pronounced *ee-no-fly-gia*.

Off

Off his base

Off his bean

Off his feet

Off his head

Off his nut: *also* Off one's nut; Off ya nut: This term appears in *The Slang Dictionary or The Vulgar Words, Street Phrases and "Fast" Expressions of High and Low Society* (London, 1884) as a term for the highest level of intoxication.

➤ **OFF ME PICKLE**

Off me trolley: *also* Off my trolley; Off of his trolley

Off my ringer

Off my woo

Off nicely

Off one's face: *also* Off ya face; Off your face

Off tap

Off the deep end

Off the leash

Off the nail: *also* Off at the nail

Off the planet

Off the wagon: *also* Fallen off the wagon; Fell off the wagon;

Under the wagon
Off to the races
Off your ass
Off your tits
Oiled: *also* Oiled up; Well-oiled
Oinophluxed

Oliver twist: Cockney rhyming slang for "pissed."

On: *also* A bit on; Bit on; Half-on; Well on: Listed in *The Slang Dictionary or The Vulgar Words, Street Phrases and "Fast" Expressions of High and Low Society* (London, 1884) as a term for mild intoxication.

On a bear-cat

On a bat: *also* Gone on a bat

On a bender: *also* A real bender; Guy on a bender; On a bar-bender; On a narrow-row bender; On a rip bender; On a spell-bound bender; On a stem-bender; On a straight road-bender

On a bout

On a brannigan

On a bus

On a campaign

On a fool's errand

On a merry-go-round

On a tear

On autopilot

On fourth: *also* On his fourth

On his ass

On his ear

On his last legs

On his way down: *also* On his way out; Well on his way; On his way to a good drunk

On instruments

On sentry: *also* On the sentry

On the batter

On the beer

On the beer scooter

On the bend: *also* On the acute bend

On the blink

On the booze

On the drink

On the floor

On the fritz

On the go: *also* Little bit on the go

On the high seas

On the lee lurch

On the ooze

On the pemishit

On the ramble

On the rampage

On the ran-tan: *also* On the randan: This term appears in *The Slang Dictionary or The Vulgar Words, Street Phrases and "Fast" Expressions of High and Low Society* (London, 1884) as a term for the highest level of intoxication.

On the razzle-dazzle

On the re-raw: *also* On the ree-raw; On the ze-raw: Appears in *The Slang Dictionary or The Vulgar Words, Street Phrases and "Fast" Expressions of High and Low Society* (London, 1884) as a term for the highest level of intoxication.

On the skyte

On the sway

On the town

On the turps

On tilt

Ona

One foot caught in a spitoon

One over the eight: This British expression is believed to stem from the bit of conventional wisdom which says that one can imbibe eight pints without appearing to be drunk.

One too many: *also* Had one too many

One's nuff: *also* Has one's nuff

Oozy

Organized: *also* All organized; Pretty well organized: Comic writer Irvin S. Cobb may have pioneered the use of this euphemism according to Manuel Prenner in his 1928 compilation in *American Speech.*

Orie-eyed

Oscillated

Ossified

Out: *also* All out; Half-out

Out buzzing low

Out cold

Out fighting foo

Out fighting the booze

Out for the count

Out getting a head of bottles

Out in bust-head society

Out in left field with a catcher's mitt on

Out jumping bush

Out like a light

Out like a lamp

Out like Lottie's eye

Out nibbling the grape

Out of commission

Out of control

Out of funds

Out of his mind: *also* Out of his mind drunk

Out of his skull

Out of his tree: *also* Out of my tree; Out yer tree

Out of it: *also* Completely out of it; Out to it

Out of key

Out of kilter

Out of my gourd

Out of one's box

Out of one's element

Out of one's head

Out of register

Out of the picture

Out of the way

Out of your face

Out on the roof

Out owl hooting

Out to lunch

Out working on the hemstitching of his straight-jacket

Over estimated his capacity: According to the San Francisco *Evening Bulletin* of Jauary 13, 1888, this term was being used in polite circles for the word "drunk."

Over the bay: *also* Half the bay over; Half the bay under: A term used by John Quincy Adams. He writes in his diary after a night of drinking that a friend "got rather over the bay."

Over the limit

Over the mark

Over the top

Overboard

Overcome

Overdone

Overloaded

Overseas

Overseen

Overserved: *also* Over served: Term popularized by comedian George Gobel in the 1950s: "I've never been drunk, but often I've been overserved."

Overset

Overshot

Oversparred: *also* Over-sparred

Overtaken

Over-wined

Owl-eyed

Owl-eyed as an owl

Owled

Owled as Mr. Hoot

Owly-eyed

Out of his latitude

Overflowing: From New York café owner Roland Elliot's 1913 collection, term for moderately drunk.

Oxycrocium: Pronounced oxy-crock-eum.

Ozone as a coon

[P]

Pabbed

Packaged: *also* Carrying a heavy package; Has a package on

Pacté: French

Padded

Pafisticated

Paggered

Paid

Painted: *also* In the paint: From New York café owner Roland Elliot's 1913 collection, term for moderately drunk.

Paintin' his nose

Painting the town red: *also* Paint the town red

Palatic: This has been defined as "very drunk" in the dialect known as Geordie which is spoken by those from the Tyneside region of England.

Palatio

Palintoshed

Palooted

Palled

Pants-shittin' drunk

Para

Paralatic: Irish

Paralytic: *also* Paraletic

Paralyzed: *also* Paralysed

Parboiled

Paris Hilton in a car

Pass out cold: *also* About to pass out; Ready to pass out

Passed

Past going

Pasted

Pealaid: South Louisianan

Pecker wavin' drunk

Peckish

Pee-eyed

Peelywally

Peevied

Peonied

Pepped: *also* Pepped up

Peppy

Pepst

Perked

Perpetual drunk

Pertish

Pervin'

Petrificated

Petrified: *also* Sure petrified

Pewtery

Phalanxed

Phfft

Picassoed

Pickled: *also* Half-pickled: Though listed by Farmer & Henley, it was regarded as American slang by the 1920s, when the term was part of a special glossary of American slang, prepared for British readers by Professor Fred Newton Scott, and republished in the *Boston Globe* on November 28, 1926.

Pickled his debts

Pickled the mustard

Piddie

Pied

Pie-eyed: *also* Pie eyed; Pye-eyed

Piffed

Pifficated

Piffle: *also* Piffled

Pifflicated

Pigeon-Eyed: From Benjamin Franklin's "Drinker's Dictionary," which says that people who hung around taverns referred to drunks as being "pigeon-eyed." Also a favorite term used by one of the co-founders of Alcoholics Anonymous, Dr. Robert H. Smith, a.k.a. Dr. Bob, who referred affectionately to alcoholics he worked with as "pigeons."

Pilfered

Pin: *also* On a merry pin: In *Blackguardiana*,1794, is the following explanation: "PIN in or to a merry pin, almost drunk, an allusion to a sort of tankard, formerly used in the north, having silver pegs or pins set at equal distances from the top to the bottom: by the rules of good fellowship, every person drinking out of one of these tankards was to swallow the quantity contained between two pins, if he drank more or less, he was to continue drinking till he ended at a pin, by this means persons unaccustomed to measure their draughts were obliged to drink the whole tankard. Hence when a person was a little elevated with liquor, he was said to have drank to a merry pin."

Pinked

Pinko

Pious: One of Ambrose Bierce's string of twenty-five synonyms for "drunk" published in *The Wasp*, August 12, 1882.

Piped

Piper-drunk: *also* Drunk as a piper; Drunk as a piper fou'; Fou' as a piper

Piper-full: *also* Full as a piper

Piper-merry

Pipped: *also* Pipped up

Pished

Pisky: Irish slang used in a song performed by Irish rock band The Pogues, "Body of an American," by Shane MacGowan:

> *The men all started telling jokes*
> *And the women they got frisky*
> *At five o'clock in the evening*
> *Every bastard there was pisky*

Piss-ass backwards

Piss-ass drunk

Piss-completed drunk

Piss'd in the brook

Pissed: *also* Bloody pissed; Half-pissed; On the piss; Pissed up; Three parts pissed

Pissed as a cricket

Pissed as a fart

Pissed as a maggot

Pissed as a mattress

Pissed as a newt

Pissed as a parrot

Pissed as a pig

➤ PISSED AS POSSUM

Pissed as a tit

Pissed in the brook

Pissed locked

Pissed mortal: Extremely drunk, in the parlance of *The Sopranos*, ca. 1999.

Pissed out his face

Pissed out of one's brains

PISSED AS POSSUM

Pissed out of one's mind

Pissed to the earlobes

Pissed to the eyeballs

Pissed up to the eyebrows

Pissin'

Pissing drunk

Pissitively possed

Pissy

Pissy-eyed

Pissy-arsed

Pissy-drunk

Pissy-eyed drunk

Pist

Pistol-shot

Pitted

➤ **PIXELATED:** *also* Pixellated: According to John Morrish writing in the *Daily Telegraph* of April 29, 2000, the term was virtually unknown in the UK until the advent of the digital age when it came to refer to an image broken into little dots or squares on a screen which came from "pixels"—picture elements.

Pixie-led

Pixilated, Originally this term meant to be under the influence of pixies. It emerged as a term in the United States in the 1840s and was used to describe those who were whimsical, confused or slightly mad. Explained by Julian Champkin of the *Daily Mail*, October 25, 2001: "She was pixilated as a newt—in other words, drunk. The word comes from fairyland, as in: 'the pixies have got at you and taken your brains away.'"

Pixy-laden

Pixy-led

Pizzacato

Placated

Plain drunk: *also* Just plain drunk; Plain old drunk

Planked: *also* Off the plank; Stiff as a plank

Planted

Plasmic

PIXELATED

Plastered: *also* Pleasantly plastered: Term which appears in a list of new youth slang in an article in the *Brooklyn Eagle* of June 19,1925: "Such Slanguage Nowadays Parents Require Lexicon To Interpret Offspring." In 1956 the Arizona Lath and Plaster Institute protested the association of this term with the state of inebriation. William F. Mitten, the institute's executive secretary told the *New York Times*: "You don't say a person is 'shingled,' 'painted' or 'landscaped,' then why say he is 'plastered'?" Walter Machos of the *Times* replied that the term in this context had nothing to do with mortar and trowel, but it came from the description of a "bird that had been riddled with shot."

Plated

Played out

Plonk: *also* Plonked

Plonkered

Ploogooed

Plootered

Plotzed: Adaptation of the Yiddish *plotz*: To burst, to explode: "I can't laugh any more or I'll 'plotz.'"

Ploughed: *also* Ploughed under; Plowed; Plowed over; Pretty well plowed; Underploughed: Defined in *The Slang Dictionary or The Vulgar Words, Street Phrases and "Fast" Expressions of High and Low Society* (London, 1884) as a term for a more intense state of beastliness that comes beyond mild intoxication and before total fuddlement.

Ploxed

Plucked

Plumb drunk

Plundered

Pluttered

Po na na'd

Pocito

Poddy

Podgy: Defined in *The Slang Dictionary or The Vulgar Words, Street Phrases and "Fast" Expressions of High and Low Society* (London, 1884) as a term for a more intense state of beastliness that comes beyond mild intoxication and before total fuddlement.

Poegaai: From South Africa. Afrikaans slang, from Dutch *poechai* for "bother" or "fuss."

Poffered

Poggled

Pogy: *also* Poegeye; Pogie

Poisoned

Polated

Poleaxed: *also* Pile-axed

Polished: *also* Polished up

Polite

Pollatic

Polled-off

Polluted: *also* Getting polluted

Poo poo'ed

Poopied

Popeyed

Popped

Porcelain-ready

Possessed

Potated

Potched

Pot-eyed

Pots on: *also* Has his pots on; In his pots

Potsed

Pot-shot

Pot-sick

Potted: *also* Potted-off

Potty

Potulent: Defined in Nathan Bailey's *New Universal English Dictionary* (1759): "Pretty much in drink."

Pot-valiant: A special breed of drunkeness defined in 1759 in Nathan Bailey's *New Universal English Dictionary* as "The adventuring upon dangerous enterprises, when a person's spirits are raised by strong liquors, which he would not dare to attempt when sober." Samuel Johnson's *Dictionary of the English Language, Second Edition*, 1755-6, defines it as "Heated with courage by strong drink."

Pot-walloped

Powdered: *also* Powdered up

Power wasted

Practically down

Praying to the porcelain god

Preaching drunk

Predicting earthquakes

Pre-hungovered

Preserved

Prestoned: From the name of a popular brand of automotive anti-freeze.

Pretty well over

Pretty well slacked

Priddy

Primed: *also* Pretty well primed; Primed up; Well primed: Defined in *The Slang Dictionary or The Vulgar Words, Street Phrases and "Fast" Expressions of High and Low Society* (London, 1884) as a term for a more intense state of beastliness that comes beyond mild intoxication and before total fuddlement.

Primed to the barrel

Primed to the muzzle

Primed to the trigger

Producing a pavement pizza

Prodded

Pruned

Psatzed

Puggled

Puggy drunk

Puking his ring up: A reference to projectile vomiting.

Pulled a Daniel Boone

Pungey

Pushed

Put in the pin

Put one on: *also* Putting one on

Put to bed with a shovel

Putrid

[Q]

Quadded

Quaffed

Quarrelsome

Quartzed

Quashed

Queer: *also* Queered

Quenched

Quick-tempered

Quilted

Quisby

[R]

Racked: *also* Racked-up

Raddled

Ragged

Raised, *also* Rais'd

Raised his monuments: *also* Rais'd his Monuments

Rammaged

Ramping mad: *also* Ramping-mad

Ranked

Rare form: *also* In rare form

Rat assed: *also* Ratarsed; Rat-arsed; Rat-assed: British slang used often in *EastEnders*, a BBC soap opera of the late 1980s. "Many get rat-arsed," says John Marcom Jr. in a review of the show in the *Wall Street Journal*.

Rat faced

Rat-legged

Rat-packed

Ratted: Writing on slang terms for drunk in the *New Statesman* for June 17, 2002, Victoria Moore explained: "One seemingly modern British expression has its roots in centuries-old slang. Since the 16th century, we have been mocking the poor rat. Similes then in common usage described people being as poor, as rank, as weak or as drunk as a rat—and from this last, we ended up with 'ratted' as well as 'rat-arsed.'"

Rattled

Ratty

Ratty as a jaybird

Raunchy

Ravaged

Razzed

Razzled

Razzle-dazzled

Reached a hundred proof

Ready: *also* Getting ready

Really

Red-eyed

Redirected

Reek-ho

Reeking: *also* Reekin' (Scottish)

Reeling

Reeling and kneeling

Reeling drunk

Reeling ripe

Reely

Re-faw

Refreshed: *also* Over refreshed

Relaxing

Religious

Rendered

Reticulum

Rich

Riding on a full tank

Right: *also* About right; Getting right; Just about right

Right down and out

Right royal: *also* Feeling right royal

Rigid

Rileyed

Ripe

Rippe

Ripped: *also* Fairly ripped; Ripped and wrecked

Ripped to the tits

Rip-roaring drunk

Ripskated

Road hugging

Roaring: *also* Roaring drunk

Roasted

Rockaputzered

Rocked

→ **ROCKET FUELED**

Rocky

Rolled off the sofa

Rolling: *also* Rolling drunk

Rooked

Roostered: "They worked hard and played hard. They got roostered (the cowboy word for 'drunk') and they gambled—one cowboy gambled away a whole herd of cattle." This from Mike Wright's *What They Didn't Teach You about the Wild West*.

Rooted

Roped

Rorty

Rosined

Rosy: *also* In a rosy glow; Rosy glow; Starting to feel rosy

Rosy about the gills

Rotten

Rotten as a chop

Round as a glass

Royal

Royally plastered

Rubbered

Ruined

Rum-dum: *also* Rum-dumb

Rummed: *also* Rummed up

Rummied

Rummy

Rung one up

Running drunk

Running on premium

Rye-soaked

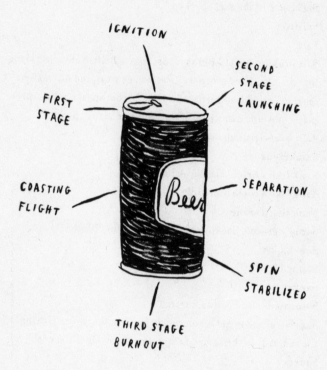

ROCKET FUELED

[S]

S.f.: *also* S.f.'ed (Shit-faced)

Sack: *also* In the sack; Sacked

Sailin'

Salt

Salt junk: Antonio Lillo says that this is British rhyming slang for "drunk." Used since the late 19th century and often shortened to "salt." It is perhaps inevitable that speakers interpret it as a punning extension of the common slang "pickled."

Salted: *also* Salted down

Salubrious

Sank like a brick: *also* Sunk like a brick

Sank like a rock: *also* Sinking like a rock

Sank like a stone

Santa's grotto: Cockney rhyming slang for "blotto."

Sap-happy

Sapped

Sappy

Saturated: *also* Really saturated

Sauced: *also* Banged up on sauce; Been in the sauce; Hitting the sauce; Into the sauce; Lost in the sauce; On the sauce

Saucey

Saw Montezuma

Sawed

Saying hello to Mr. Armitage: The origins of this term have been obscured by time; but it is worth noting that it is also used as bar slang for urinating, as in "I have to go and say hello to Mr. Armitage."

Scammered: This term appears in *The Slang Dictionary or The Vulgar Words, Street Phrases and "Fast" Expressions of High and Low Society* (London, 1884) as a term for the highest level of intoxication.

Scooped

Scattered

Schicker: *also* Had a couple of shickers; On the shikker; Schickered; Shicer; Shick; Shicker; Shickered; Shikker; Shikkered: According to S. B. Flexner, "shikker," "shicker" and "schickered" all come from the Yiddish word for drunk, *shikker*.

Schindlers: According to Antonio Lillo, this British term is an abbreviation of the rhyming slang "Schindler's List" (from the title of the 1993 film directed by Steven Spielberg) meaning "pissed."

Schizzed-out

Schlitzed

Schlockkered

Schlonkered

Schmaltzed

Schnapped: *also* Schnapp'd

Schnockered: *also* Schnockkered; Shnockered

Schnoggered

Schtumphy

Schwacked

Scoobied

Scooped

Scoopered

Scorched

Scotch mist: British, as in "Are you Scotch mist, mate?", which is rhyming slang for "pissed." Courtesy of Antonio Lillo.

Scotched

Scrambled

Scrambled to the gills

Scraped

Scratched

Scraunched

Screaming drunk

Screeching: *also* Screeching drunk

Screwed: *also* Half-screwed: A July 9, 1859 poem in *Punch* entitled "A Chapter on Slang" contains the line "For brutally drunk, he's as Screwed as old Nick."

➤ **SCREWED TO THE CARPET**

Screwy: *also* Screwy drunk

Scronched

Scrooched up

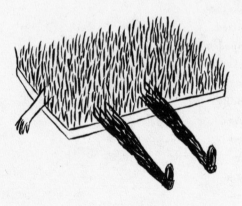

SCREWED TO THE CARPET

Scrooped

Scudded: U.S. Military slang from the first Gulf War, refer-
ring to the Iraqi Scud missiles that sometimes fly around
aimlessly and fall anywhere.

Scuppered

Scuttered

➤ **SEAFARING**

Seasick

Seasoned

Seeing bears: *also* Seeing the bears

Seeing by twos

SEA FARING

Seeing double

Seeing the French king

Seeing the snakes

Seeing the yellow star

Seeing triple

Seeing two moons: *also* Seeing a flock of moons

Segued

Sell one's senses: *also* Has Sold his Senses; Sold his senses

Semibousie: *also* Semibousy: Listed in John Ash's 1795 *New and Complete Dictionary of the English Language* as an obsolete term for "half drunk."

Sent

Served: *also* Served-up

Set-up

Several slugs behind the midriff

Sewed: *also* Sewed up; Sewn up: "Sewed up" appears in *The Slang Dictionary or The Vulgar Words, Street Phrases and "Fast" Expressions of High and Low Society* (London, 1884) as a term for the highest level of intoxication.

Shackled

Shagg

Shagged

Shaggy

Shaking a cloth in the wind: Found in the novel *Mutiny on the Bounty* describing the ship's surgeon, known as Old Bacchus, whose "normal state was what sailors call 'in the wind' or 'shaking a cloth'…"

Shaky: *also* Getting shaky; So shaky he couldn't pour whiskey into a barrel with the end knocked out

Shamming sober: The term was volunteered by a man who identified himself as "A Late Fleet Streeter" in a letter to the *Sporting Times*, April 23, 1883. Fleet Street was the main street for newspapers and journalists in London, from the early 19th century through most of the 20th century. Fleet Street journalists were known for their drinking.

➤ SHAMROCKED

Shattered

Shaved: *also* Half shaved; Half-shaved

Shedded: *also* Sheded: As in "My shed has collapsed taking most of the fence with it."

Sheet in the wind: *also* A sheet in the wind's eye; Both sheets in the wind; Both sheets to the wind; Four sheets to the wind; Nine sheets to the wind; Sheet and a half to the wind; Sheets in the wind; Six sails to the wind; Six sheets to the wind; Three sheets in the shade; Three sheets in the wind and the other

SHAMROCKED

one flapping; Three sheets to the wind; Three sheets to the wind's eye; Two sheets to the wind: This nautical expression is not based on sheets meaning sails but rather on the meaning of sheet as a rope attached to the lower corners of a sail that controls the angle at which it is set, according to *Brewer's Dictionary of Phrase and Fable* and other sources. The expression famously appears in Charles Dickens's *Dombey and Son*: "Captain Cuttle looking, candle in hand, at Bunsby more attentively, perceived that he was three sheets in the wind, or, in plain words, drunk."

Shellacked: In an article on slang by cartoonist H.T. Webster entitled "They Don't Speak Our Language," *Forum and Century*, December, 1933, this term was cited along with other terms for "drunk," including "shined," "jingled" and "petrified." This is clearly an American contribution as it appears in a list of new slang entitled "Slanguage, 1929," published widely in U.S. newspapers including *The Baltimore Sun* of January 9, 1929.

Shellacked the goldfish bowl

Sherbetty

Shews his hobnails

Shined: *also* Has a shine on; Shined up

Shiny: *also* Shiny drunk

Shipwrecked

Shit babied

Shit bombed

Shit-faced: *also* Shatfaced; Shitfaced; Shifassed ("Shit-faced" in slurvian)

Shit hammered

Shit licked

Shit wrecked

Shithoused: *also* Shit housed; Got a shithouse on

Shitty

Shitty-ass-nasty

Shoe the goose: *also* To shoe the goose

Shot: *also* About shot; Getting shot; Half-shot: An old term given new currency with the popularity of the shooter—defined herewith: Shooter. (Drink) (1) Straight shot meant for consuming in one gulp. (2) House drink that is usually sweet and easy to consume quickly. These shooters are common to summer beach bars and often feature a fruit liqueur, such as DeKuyper Peachtree Schnapps, or Southern Comfort, or tequila. These drinks often have names that are as wild as their formulas. The Beachcomber, a contemporary newspaper from the Delaware coast, contained a "shooter survey" rating such libations as the Blood Clot, Midnight at the Oasis, 57 Chevy with Hawaiian Plates, Sex on the Beach, the Russian Quaalude, Deep Throat, the Chocolate Virgin, Daphnie Divine's Deluxe Dixie Daiquiri and The Bay Bridge Commuter Shooter. For a "State-Of-The-Art" in the 2005 issue of Bartender magazine, there was a formula for a "Pierced Nipple."

Shot away

Shot down

Shot full of holes

Shot in the arm

Shot in the mouth

Shot in the neck: John Russell Bartlett lists it in his *Dictionary Of Americanisms*, 1848, adding that it is a Southern term.

Shot in the wrist

Shot to the eyebrows

Shot-up

Showing his booze

Showing his tipsiness

Showing it: *also* A-showin' it; It's showing on him; Just showing signs

Shredded

Shwilly

Sidewalk lickin' drunk

Sidewayed

Sideways: "Is a Wine-Soaked Film Too, Er, Rosé?" Mireya Navarro asked in the *New York Times* of February 20, 2005, whether the movie 2004 movie "Sideways" was really about an alcoholic, rather than a simple wine lover who sometimes lost control, pointing out that in the book on which the movie was based "sideways" is used as synonym for "drunk."

Silly: *also* Acting silly; pretty silly; silly drunk

Simmerin'

Singed

Sir Richard has taken off his Considering Cap: *also* Been too free with Sir Richard: In "Franklin's 'Drinkers Dictionary' Again," *American Speech*, February 1940, Louise Pound speculated that this was a reference to "Sir Richard Rum, so called in New England."

Sizzled

Skeerewy drunk

Skew-whiff

Skinned

Skitted

Skulled

Skunk drunk

Skunked

Skunky

Slam hammered

Slambasted

Slammed: *also* Half-slammed

Slap drunk

Slap-ass drunk

Slathered

Slaughtered

Slewed: *also* Half-slewed: John Russell Bartlett in his *Dictionary Of Americanisms*, 1848, lists it and defines it as "Moderately drunk." Bartlett says it is a common Americanism but also appears in Yorkshire, England.

Slewy

Slick

Slickered

Slightly less than perpendicular

Slightly tightly

Slippery: The *Cleveland Herald*, May 1, 1849, carries this item: "Yer drunk again, hey?" "No my love, (hiccup) not drunk but slippery. The fact is, my dear, somebody has been rubbing the bottom of my boots (hiccup) till they are smooth as glass."

Slipping

Slitted

Slobbered

Slopped: *also* Half-slopped; Slopped over; Slopped to the ears; Slopped up

Slopped to the gills

Sloppo: This could be author Stephen King's coinage as the only place it has been spotted is his novel *The Stand* when a character named Ralph is told that alcoholism is a disease. Ralph responds: "Disease, my ass. It's getting sloppo, that's what it is."

Sloppy: *also* Sloppy drunk; Sloppy like soup

Sloshed: *also* Sloshed to the ears

Slotted

Sloughed

Slozzled

Slued

Slugged

Slurks

Slushed: *also* Slushed-up

Smacked up

Smashed: This could relate to an early drink called the "Smasher." John Russell Bartlett in his *Dictionary Of Americanisms*, 1848, lists this as one of "the many various compounds or mixtures of spiritous liquors and wines, served up in fashionable bar rooms in the United States." Some other drinks listed by Bartlett include: Tip and Ty, Fiscal Agent, Polk and Dallas, Shambro, Jewett's Fancy, Slingflip, Ropee, Porteree, Tog, Deacon, Sargent, Moral Suasion, I.O.U., Arrack Punch, Chain Lightning, Sifter, Stone Wall, Silver Top, Vox Populi and the Rochelle Cobbler. The only names, of the many on the list, which still have currency are the Plain Mint Julep and the Cocktail.

Smashed out of his mind

Smashed to the gills

Smeared

Smeekit

Smelling of the cork: *also* Smelled the big cork

Smitten by the grape

Smoked

Smothered

Smuckered

Smurfed up

Snackered

Snaked

Snakes hissed: Rhyming slang for "pissed."

Snapped: *also* Half-snapped

Snapt: John Russell Bartlett quotes from a work entitled *Major Jones's Courtship* by Joseph Jones, 1852: "I like to forgot to tell you 'bout cousin Pete. He got snapt on egg-nog when he heard of my engagement."

Snatch't

Snatered: Irish

Snerred

Snicker-doodled

Sniffed the barmaid's apron

Sniffy

Snobbled: Welsh

Snockered: *also* Snockkered; Snockkered up; Snonkered

Snoot full: *also* Getting a snootful; Got a snootful; Has a snootful

Snooted

Snoozamorooed

Snot-flying drunk

Snot-slinging

Snotted

Snozzled

Snubbed

Snuffy

Snug

So

So drunk he couldn't hit the ground with his hat in three tries

So drunk he started seein' things that ain't there

Soaked: *also* In soak; Soak'd; Soaked his face; Soaked-up; Soaken; Well-soaked

Soaked to the gills

Soako

Soapy-eyed

Sobbed

Sober impaired

Socked

Sodden: *also* Sodden-drunk

Soft: *also* Getting soft

Soggy

Some-drunk

Sopped

Sopping: *also* Sopping wet

Soppy

Sopsy: As defined on the website Urban Dictionary: "Sopsy is used to define a specific state between the different levels of drunkenness. It's when you're past sober, but not quite tipsy: 'I drank 2 rum and Cokes to get me started, but after half an hour I found I hadn't gotten myself past sopsy.'"

Sore footed

Soshed

So-so

Sostinko'd

Sotally tober

Sotted: *also* Sot drunk; sottish

Sotto

Soul in soak: *also* Has one's soul in soak; One's soul in soak

Soupy

Soused: *also* Fully soused; Getting soused; Half-soused; Really soused; Soused as a pig's face; Soused to the ears; Soused up: Comedian W.C. Fields played "Egbert Sousé" [pronounced "soo-ZAY"] in the film "The Bank Dick," which is almost certainly a play on this synonym.

Soused to the gills

Southern comforted

Southern-fried

Sow-drunk

Sozzled

Sozzly

Spaced out

Spaghetti-headed

Spak: Pidgin English

Spangled

Spanked

Spannered

Sparkling like the 4th of July

Spaz-ratted

Speared

Speechless

Spent

Spiffed

Spifficated

Spiffilo

Spiffled

Spiflicated

Spirited

Spliced

Sploshed

Splotched

Spoke with his friend

Sponge-eyed

Sponge-headed

Spongelled

Spoony: *also* Spoony drunk

Spotty

Spreed: *also* Gone on a spree; On a spree; On the spree;
Spreed up; Spreeish

Sprinkled

Sprung: *also* Cup-sprung; Half-sprung; Well sprung

Squamed

Squared

Squashed: *also* Completely squashed

Squiffed: *also* Squiffed out

Squiffy: In one mock conjugation from the satirical magazine *Fun*, August 7, 1878, it is stated that "squiffy" is the past tense of "Thou are all mops and brooms."

Squiffy-eyed

➡ **SQUIRRELLY**

Squished

Staggering: *also* Beginning to stagger; Staggering around; Staggering drunk; Staggerish; Staggers; Staggery

Stale: *also* Stale drunk

Starched

Starchery

Starchy

Stark drunk

Starry-eyed

Starting to show his drink

Stary-eyed

Staying late at the office

Steady

Steamboats: Defined in *The Dictionary of the Scots Language* as "a picturesque if somewhat inexplicable word for drunk: 'Look at the state of him—steamboats again!'"

Steamed: *also* Steamed-up; Steamin; Steaming; Under full steam

Steampigged

Steeped

Stewed: *also* Half-stewed; In a stew; Stew'd; Stewed up

Stewed as a fresh boiled owl

Stewed like a prune

SQUIRRELY

Stewed to the balls: In John O'Hara's novel *BUtterfield 8*, first published in 1935, the lead female character wishes to rid herself of a woman who has sat at her luncheon table. They get into slang. The intruder asks what her friends say when they have had too much to drink. The lead female replies, "I was stewed to the balls last night." The intruder leaves in a huff.

Stewed to the ears

Stewed to the eyebrows

Stewed to the gills: Perhaps the most common of the phrases using the word "gills," which is slang for neck, meaning he/she is extremely drunk with alcohol reaching from his/her stomach to his/her neck (or "gills").

Sticked

Stiff: *also* Half-stiff

Stiff as a carp

Stiff as a goat

Stiff as a ramrod

Stiff as a Ring-bolt

Stiffed

Stiffer than a cucumber

Stiffo

Still on his feet

Stimulated

Stink

Stinkarooed

Stinking: *also* Stinken; Stink'in; Stinking drunk

Stinko

Stinky: *also* Stinky drunk

Stitched: *also* Stitch'd

Stoatin

Stocious: *also* Stotious: Victoria Moore, writing in the *New Statesman* of June 17, 2002, on terms for drunk suggests: "The Irish have stocious, which is how a thickly speaking drunk might pronounce 'atrocious'"

Stocked-up

Stoked

Stokered

Stolichnyed

Stolled

Stolling

Stonato: Italian

Stone cold drunk

Stoned

Stoned out of his mind

Stoned to the gills

Stonkered: "It's a bit rich for a man who got famously stonkered at a lap-dancing club five years ago to be lecturing the rest of us on binge drinking," was the reaction to a 2008 campaign against binge drinking by Australian Prime Minister Kevin Rudd, from *Sydney Morning Herald* columnist Miranda Devine.

Stonkin

Stooped

Stottin

Stove in

Stozzled

Straddled-legged

Street-loaded

Stretched

Striped

Strong

Strontzat: From Flemish

Stubbed: *also* Stubb'd

Stuccoed

Studying snakes

Stuffed

Stuk in men kloten: From Flemish

Stumble-drunk

Stumblin'

Stung

Stunked

Stunko

Stunned

Stupefied

Stupid

Stupidlegged

Suck: *also* Sucked; Sucky: In *Blackguardiana*, 1794, is the
definition, "SUCK, strong liquor of any sort...SUCKY: drunk;
to suck the monkey." "Monkey," Caufield explains, "is a straw
or small tube used to drink liquor from a cask."

Suffering from the flu

Sugar-smacked

Sun in the eyes: *also* Has the sun in one's eyes; Got the sun in
the eyes; With the sun in one's eyes

Sunk

Sure 'nuff drunk

Suttle

Swacked: *also* Swacked out; Swacko

Swallied

Swallowed a hare: In *Blackguardiana*, 1794: "HARE, he has
swallowed a hare, he is drunk, more probably a hair which
requires watering down."

Swallowed a tavern token

Swamped: *also* Swampt

Swatched

Swatted

Swattled

Swazzled

Sweatin' Stoli

Sweaved

Sweet

Swerved

Swiffy

Swigged

Swiggled

Swilled: *also* Swilled up

Swillo

➤➤ **SWIMMING DRUNK**

Swine-drunk: *also* Drunk as swine

Swiney

Swinnied

Swiped

Swipy: "Swipy" is listed in *The Slang Dictionary or The Vulgar Words, Street Phrases and "Fast" Expressions of High and Low Society* (London, 1884) as a term for a more intense state of beastliness that comes beyond mild intoxication and before total fuddlement.

Switchery

Switchy

Swivelly

Swizzled

Swozzled

SWIMMING DRUNK

[T]

Tacked

Tacky

Tacoed

Tajado

Taken a segue

Taken a shard: *also* To take a shard

Taken in some o-be-joyful

Taking it easy

Talking loud

➤ **TALKING TO EARL ON THE BIG WHITE PHONE:** *also*

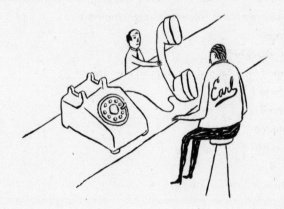

TALKING TO EARL ON
THE BIG WHITE PHONE

Called Earl on the big white phone

Talking to Jamie Moore

Talking to Jim Beam: An allusion to the popular brand of bourbon.

Talking to Ralph on the big white phone: *also* Called Ralph on the big white phone

Tangled

➤ **TANGLE-LEGGED**: *also* Tangle-footed; Tanglelegged

Tap-shackled

Tanked: *also* Fully tanked; Getting tanked up; Half-tanked; Piss-tanked; Tanked out; Tanked to the wide; Tanked up; Tanked-up; Tanky: Noted by H. L. Mencken in *The American Language*, but also listed as one of the more popular terms for drunk during the Vietnam War, in Gregory R. Clark's *Words of the Vietnam War*, and given new popularity by Steve Dallas in the late lamented "Bloom County" comic strip.

Tanned

Tap-shackled

Tapped; *also* Tapped out; Tapped the admiral

Tashered

Tatered

Tattooed

Taverned

Taxed

Tean

Ted

Teed: *also* Bit teed; Bit teed up; Getting teed up; Tead up; Teed off; Teed up

Teetered

Teeth under

Temulent: *also* State of temulency; Temulentious; Temulen-

TANGLE LEGGED

tive: This term appears in Noah Webster's 1806 *Dictionary* and is defined as "intoxicated, fuddled, drunk."

Ten feet tall and bullet proof

Tepo

Terminated

That way

Thawed

The King is his cousin

The Malt is above the water

The malt is above the wheat

The way he spraddled down the street you'd think walkin' was a lost art

There

There with both feet: *also* Got there with both feet

There with the goods

There with what it takes

Thick-headed

Thick-legged

Thick-lipped

Thick-tongued

Thirsty

Thora-Hirded

Thrashed

Three bricks short of a load

Three-parts seven-eighths: A term invoked in a letter from "D.T." to the *Sporting Times*, April 22, 1893, as a common term (along with "toxey-boozey") used "among the members of our little community" which calls itself "Inebriates' Retreat."

Throttled

Throw down

Throwed off

Tickeyboo

Tiddly: also Bit tiddley; Tiddled: Genteel British slang for "drunk" which may be derived from early rhyming slang for drinks: "tiddlywinks," or is simply onomatopoetic.

Tiddleywinks

Tied one on: *also* Really tied one on; Sure tied one on

Tiffled

Tight: *also* Full tight; Little tight: "Tight," meaning drunk, is "a tailor's slang expression that has survived from the early 19th century, equating the tightness of military dress with drunkenness" according to the book *British Military Spectacle From The Napoleonic Wars Through The Crimea* by Scott Hughes Myerly, Harvard University Press. "Tight" appears in *The Slang Dictionary or The Vulgar Words, Street Phrases and "Fast" Expressions of High and Low Society* (London, 1884) as a term for mild intoxication.

Tight as a brassiere

Tight as a drum: *also* Tighter than a drum

Tight as a fart

Tight as a goat

Tight as a mink

Tight as a tick

Tight as Andronicus: *also* As tight as Andronicus: From Shakespeare's Titus Andronicus, a Noble Roman general who has won a long war against the Goths but lost many of his sons in battle. Although he is at first a reasonable man, events of the play transform him into a madman bent on bloody revenge.

Tight as the bark on a tree

Tight-wadded

Tighter than a boot

Tighter than a Woolworth sock

Tile counting

Time traveling

Tin hatted: *Also* Tin hats

Tin top tippled

Tinned

Tinted: From New York café owner Roland Elliot's 1913 collection, term for being mildly drunk.

Tip merry

Tipium grove: *also* In tipium grove

Tipped

Tipping

Tippled: *also* On a tipple

Tipply

Tippsified

Tippy

Tipsy: *also* Bit tipsy; Real tipsy; Half-tipsy; Tipsey: John Ash's 1795 *New and Complete Dictionary of the English Language* says it is derived from "tipple." The term appears in Noah Webster's 1806 *Dictionary* as "almost drunk or fuddled, merry, drunk," and is euphemistic enough to name a free taxi service for the alcoholically impaired, as in Aspen, Colorado's "Tipsy Taxi." It refers to being less than being fully drunk, as attested to in a *Daily Evening Bulletin*, San Francisco, CA, headline for April 7, 1857, "He Was Not Drunk But Only Tipsy." The earliest US use, in *The Arkansas Gazette*, June 6, 1832, alluded to a British member of Parliament as "The tipsy member."

Tip-top

Tired

Tired and emotional: *also* Tired and emotional as a newt: Patrick Marnham writes in *The Private Eye Story*, a history of the popular British weekly, *Private Eye*: "It was quite impossible in those days for the press to say that a cabinet minister was drunk. Fleet Street instead used synonyms. *Private Eye*

thereupon published a spoof Foreign Office memo giving the
translation in French, Italian, German and Russian for the
words 'tired,' 'overwrought,' 'expansive,' 'overworked,' 'colour-
ful' and 'emotional.' One of the most famous *Eye* phrases, 'tired
and emotional,' had been born. It is still used by the magazine
as evidenced by this line from a 2006 issue: Harry was 'fired up.
He'd been drinking and was *tired and emotional*.' The use of the
phrase has extended well beyond the magazine."

Tishy

Tit tickled

Titled

Tits up

Tizzed

To burn with a low blue flame

Toddy stricken

To let the finger ride the thumb

To need a reef taken in

To see the devil: *also* Seeing the devil

To' up from the flo' up

Toasted

Toastified

Toasty

 TOE-UP

Toilet huggin' drunk

Tol-lol

Tongue-tied: *also* Tounge-ty'd

Tonks

Too far north

Too intimate with the striped pig

Too many clothes on the wind

Too numerous to mention

Toodled

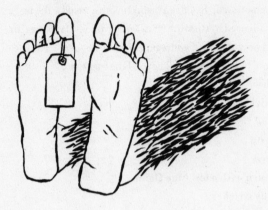

T⏀E VP

Toonst

Tooted: *also* On a toot

Toozered

Toped

Toper

Top-heavy: *The Slang Dictionary or The Vulgar Words, Street Phrases and "Fast" Expressions of High and Low Society* (London, 1884) lists the term as a more intense state of beastliness that comes beyond mild intoxication and before total inebriation.

Top-loaded

Topped: *also* Top'd; Topped off ; Topped off his antifreeze; Topped up; Topper

Toppy: From New York café owner Roland Elliot's 1913 collection, term for being mildly drunk.

Topsy: *also* Got topsy

Topsy-boozy: *also* Topsy-boosy

Topsy Turvey

Tore back

Tore up: *also* Tore up from the floor up; Tore-up

Torn: *also* Torn up

Torn off the frame

Torqued

Torrid

Torrid-tossed

Toshed

Tossed

Tosticated

Tostified

Totaled: *also* Totaled out; Totalled

Totally drunk

Totted

Touched; *also* Rather touched; Touched off

Touched as a boiled owl

Tow up

Towed

Towered: Eponymous term created in honor of the habits of the late U.S. Senator John Tower of Texas. Used in *Roll Call*, March 13-19, 1989: "Let's go to the Tune Inn and get Towered." The Tune Inn was, and still is, a Washington watering hole.

Toxed

Toxey-boozey: Invoked in a letter from "D.T." to the *Sporting Times*, April 22, 1893, as a common term used among the members of a little community which the writer claims was known as "Inebriates' Retreat."

Toxic

Toxicated

Toxified

Toxy

Trammeled; *also* Trammel'd

Trampled

Translated

Trashed; *also* Trashed basted; Trashed out of my bracket; Trashed out of one's gourd

Treed

Trimmed down

Tripped up

Tripping: *also* Taking a trip

Troattered

➤➤ **TROLL-EYED**

Trolleyed: *also* Trollied: Writing on slang terms for drunk in the *New Statesman*, June 17, 2002, Victoria Moore wrote: "Trolleyed is a Nineties word. My slang dictionary relates it to the phrase 'off one's trolley' but how can we be sure? Couldn't it just as likely come from students on nights out, who (when they're not stealing souvenir traffic cones and road signs) always seem to end up racing around in a supermarket trolley? Or from supermarket trolleys, which are as cranky to steer as someone who's had a few? Or could it be another variation on 'f***ed,' from the rhyming slang 'trolley and truck?'"

Troubled

Trounced

Trousered

T.U.B.B. (abbreviation for "tits up—but breathing"): This term was reported by C.W. Sande, M.D., an emergency room physician and surgeon who heard it from his paramedics, in a letter to the author, July 13, 1983.

TROLL EYED

Tubed

Tumbled down the sink

Tumbling: *also* Tumbling drunk

Tuned: *also* Tuned up; Tuned up a little

Turned on

Turugiddy

Twatted

Tweeked

Tweeter-myer'd

Twisted

Twisting in the wind

[U]

U.I.: Under the influence

Ugly

Ugly drunk

Umbriacco: *also* Umbriago: Italian

Unable to scratch oneself

Unbalanced

Uncorked

Under: *also* About to go under; Down under; Going under; Half-under; Slightly under; Well under

Under full sail

Under the afluence of incohol

Under the influence: *also* Getting under the influence: A seemingly modern term, but it is listed by Farmer & Henley in *Slang and its Analogues*, 1890-1904.

Under the table

Under the weather

Underway: *also* Getting under way; Well under way

Unglued

Unk-dray: Pig latin, as in "Ed-fray is unk-dray as a ord-lay"

(Fred is drunk as a lord.")

Unsensed

Unsober

Unsteady

Untidy

Unwell: Lew Golin writes about drunken euphemisms in the *Toronto Sun*, "One of the more interesting circumlocutions is "unwell," as in *Jeffrey Barnard Is Unwell*, a 2003 play about the *London Spectator* writer whose column is sometimes missing because its author is somewhat the worse for drink."

Up a stump

Up a tree

Up in one's hat: *also* Up in his hat: "Up in his hat" was employed by James Joyce in *Ulysses*.

Up on blocks

Up the pole

Up to the ears

Up to the eyeballs

Up to the gills: *also* Full to the gills

Up to this

Upholstered

Uplaid

Uppish

Uppity

Upsey

Upside down

Useless

[V]

Valiant

Vapor-locked

Varnished

➤ VEGETABLE
Very
Very much disguised
Very relaxed
Vinolence
Vision-impaired
Vitrified: From New York café owner Roland Elliot's 1913 collection, term for completely drunk.

➤ VULCANIZED

VEGETABLE

VULCANIZED

[W]

Waazey

Waa-zooed

Walking calamity

Walking on his cap badge

Walking tall

Wall-eyed

Wallpapered

Wam-bazzled

Wanked

Wankered

Wapsed down: Edmund Wilson's 1927 list reports that this is "a rural expression applied to crops that have been laid low by a storm."

Warm: This was a common term for drunk in Philadelphia in the 1860s according to the *North American and United States Gazette* of May 21, 1867.

Warming up

Warped

Washed

Wassailed out; *also* Wassailed up; Wholly-wassailed

Wasted: *also* Getting wasted; Got wasted

Wasted his Paunch

Watching the ant races

Watered

Waterlogged

Water-soaked: *also* Water-soaken

Waving a flag of defiance

Waxed

Wazzed

Wazzocked

Weak jointed
Wearin' sake goggles
Wearing a barley cap
 **WEARING A BIG HAT**

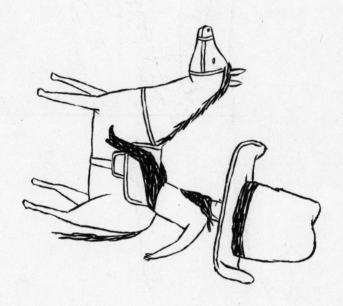

WEARING A BIG HAT

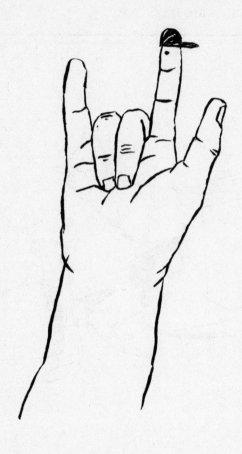

WEARING THE SMALL CAP

➤ WEARING THE SMALL CAP

Wearing the wobbly boots: *also* Got my wobbly boots on; Got the wobbly boots on; Wearing a wobbly boot: Australian

Weary: *also* Very weary

Weaving

Welched

Well away

Well beyond

Well heeled

Well jointed

Well to Live

Well wrapped

Wellied

Wet: *also* All wet; Got wet; So wet he ripples

Wet as a wanker's whistle

Wet both his eyes

Wet within

Wet-handed

Wettish

Whacked: *also* Wacked; Whack-assed; Whacked out

Whaled

What the fucked

What-nosed: *also* Whackywhat-nosed

Whazood

Wheelchaired

Wheeled

Whiffled

Whipcat

Whipped

Whipsey

Whiskied: *also* Whiskeyfied; Whiskey-frisky; Whiskey-raddled; Whiskey-shot

Whistle drunk: Presumably a reference to one's whistle which one wets drinking. Benjamin Franklin once wrote of a man whose life was consumed by alcohol: "He has paid dear, very dear for his whistle."

Whistled: "Let's...drink the other cup to wet our whistles, and so sing away all sad thoughts," from Izaak Walton's *The Compleat Angler*, 1653.

Whittin stewed

Whittled

Whittled as a penguin

Whooshed: *also* Wooshed

Whopped up

Wicked retarded: Boston

Wide

Wide-eyed and legless

Wild

Williamed: Belfast

Wilted

Wined

Wine-potted

Winey: Listed in *The Slang Dictionary or The Vulgar Words, Street Phrases and "Fast" Expressions of High and Low Society* (London, 1884) as a term for mild intoxication.

Wingdinged

Wing-heavy

Winterized

Wiped: *also* Wiped out; Wiped over

Wire faced

Wired: *also* Wired to a bottle; Wired to the tits; Wired up; Wired-up

Wise

Witched up
With the fairies: *also* Away with the fairies
With the topgallant sails out: *also* He's got his Top Gallant
Sails out
With too many cloths in the wind
With too much sail: *also* Carrying too much sail
Wobble
Wobbly: *also* Bit wobbly; Wobbly kneed
Woggled
Woggly
Wollied
Wombled: *also* Wamble crop'd; Womble-ty-cropt
Woofy
Woozy: *also* Getting kind of woozy; Getting woozy; Got woozy;
Kind of woozy; Little woozy; Slightly woozy; Whoozy; Woosy;
Woozey
Worked
Wormed: The belief that alcohol kills worms in the stomach
furnished yet another convenient excuse for having a drink.
Wounded
Wrapped up in warm flannel
Wrecked
Written off

[X]

➤ X FILED

[Y]

Yappish: *also* Yappy; Yaupish; Yaupy

X-FILED

➤➤ **YDRUNKEN**
Yellow fever
Yoimashita: Japanese slang term for paralytically drunk which
has appeared in stories about British soccer fans in Japan.

YDRUNKEN

[Z]

Zambonied: A reference to the Zamboni ice re-surfacing machine.

Zapped

Zeroed

Ziced

Zig-zag: *also* Zagged; Zigzag; Zigzagged

Zin Zagged

Zin Zan

Zinged

➤ **ZIPPED**

ZIPPED

Zippered

Zippen

Zissified

Zombied

Zombified

➤ **ZONED**

Zonged

Zonked: *also* Zonkers; Zonked out

Zooted

Zorba'd: Used since at least the late 1990s. According to Antonio Lillo: "I first heard it in Edinburgh in 1998: 'You

ZONED

shut up. You're fucking Zorba'd.' It derives from *Zorba the Greek*, rhyming with 'leak.' Hence *Zorba the Greeked*, meaning 'leaked' (in the sense of 'drunk')."

Zorked

Zozzled

Zui: A Chinese word which, according to *The Politics of Chinese Language and Culture: The Art of Reading Dragons* by Bob Hodge and Kam Louie, "is more like 'blotto' than 'drunk.'

WORKS CITED

"A to Z Guide to Street Slang from the 1700s; A Whapper Tried a Goat's Jig with a Wagtail but He Was Milking the Pigeon Because His Sugar Stick Was Kickerapoo." *The People*, London, England: 2004:8.

Abel, Ernest L. *Alcohol: Wordlore and Folklore*. Buffalo, New York: Prometheus Books, 1987.

Allen, Irving Lewis. *The City in Slang: New York Life and Popular Speech*. New York: Oxford, 1993.

Allen, Irving Lewis. *The Language of Ethnic Conflict: Social Organization and Lexical Culture*. New York: Columbia University Press, 1983.

Allen, Irving Lewis. *Unkind Words: Ethnic Labeling from Redskin to Wasp*. New York: Bergin & Garvey, 1990.

Anti-Dram. "Cheap Drunkenness." *American Mechanics' Magazine: Containing Useful Original Matter, On Subjects Connected With Manufactures, The Arts And Sciences* 19 Mar. 1825.

"At a Late Meeting of the 'Superior' Clergy, It is Stated that the Health of the Bishop of London was Drunk 'in Solumn Silence.'" *The Satirist; or, the Censor of the Times* 24 May 1835.

Ash, John. *The New And Complete Dictionary Of The English Language...To Which Is Prefixed A Comprehensive Grammar.* Second edition, 2 vols. London: printed for Vernor and Hood, 1795.

Bailey, Nathan. *The New Universal English Dictionary...To Which Is Added, A Dictionary Of Cant Words.* The fourth edition, carefully corrected by Mr. Buchanan. London: 1759.

Bain, Charlie. "NEVER GET A TWO-POT SCREAMER MULLERED; Slang Gets New Dictionary" (1737). *The Mirror* 23 Sept. 1997.

Bartlett, John Russell. *Dictionary Of Americanisms: A Glossary Of Words And Phrases, Usually Regarded As Peculiar To The United States.* New York: 1848.

Batcholder, Roger. "Cheerio! American Slang Is Far Better Than England's; Mr. Wodehouse, Past Master of It in His Stories, Says So." *The World* 22 Mar. 1922.

Beauclerk, Charles. *Nell Gwynn: Mistress to a King.* New York: Atlantic Monthly Press, 2003.

Behan, Brendan. *Borstal Boy.* Boston: D.R. Godine, 1982.

Berrey, Lester V. and Van den Bark, Melvin. *The American Thesaurus Of Slang; A Complete Reference Book Of Colloquial Speech.* New York: Crowell, 1953.

Berson, Joel S. "The source for Benjamin Franklin's 'The Drinkers Dictionary' (And was it Mather Byles?)." *American Speech* 81.2 (Summer, 2006).

Bertram, Anne. *In A Pig's Eye—The Dictionary Of Country Jawing.* New York: Gramercy Books, 1997.

Bierce, Ambrose. "25 Synonyms For Drunk," *The Wasp* 12 Aug. 1882.

"Blue Devils." *The World Of Fashion And Continental Feuilletons 62.* London, England: Wednesday, 1 Jul. 1829.

Bogira, Steve. "Du Jour: Lots of Nice Ways to Say You Were Stinking Drunk." *Chicago Tribune* 1 Jan. 1979.

"Booze." *The Sporting Times* 21 April 1883, and letters in response in the issue of 28 April 1883. The first article contained 34 terms.

Brewer, I.E Cobham. *Dictionary Of Phrase And Fable.* 1898.

Brier, Bud. "Under The Rose." *Boston Globe* 7 Feb. 1896.

Brown, Pete. *Man Walks into a Pub* (which begins with an impressive list of 120 synonyms for "drunk").

Bushman's Drunk, The. *The Country Gentleman, Sporting Gazette, Agricultural Journal and The Man About Town.* London, England: 15 Oct. 1898.

"Can you Speak da lingo? OUR A-Z GUIDE TO THE ENGLISH LANGUAGE TODAY." *The People* 13 Jan. 2008.

Caulfield, James. *Blackguardiana: Or, A Dictionary Of Rogues, Bawds, Pimps, Whores, Pickpockets, Shoplifters...Illustrated With Eighteen Portraits Of The Most Remarkable Professors In Every Species Of Villainy. Interspersed With Many Curious Anecdotes, Cant Terms, Flash Songs, &C. The Whole Intended To Put Society On Their Guard Against Depredators.* London: 1794. (The date of this very rare work was hitherto unknown but has been ascertained in a recently digitized catalog in which the date is clearly established. The catalog appears in the Gale database *Eighteenth Century Collections Online* along with *Blackguardiana.* The catalog is listed under Edgerton in this bibliography.)

Champkin, Julian. "Oh, My Word! Are You Antsy, Eggy Or Is Life Just Cushty? And Do You Need A Dictionary To Find Out What It All Means?" *Daily Mail* 25 Oct. 2001.

"City Christmas Jollities." *The Satirist; or, the Censor of the Times* 30 Dec. 1832.

Clark, Gregory R. *Words of the Vietnam War: The Slang, Jargon, Abbreviations, Acronyms, Nomenclature, Nicknames, Pseudonyms, Slogans, Specs, Euphemisms, Double-Talk, Chants, and Names and Places of the Era of United States Involvement in Vietnam.* Jefferson, NC: McFarland, 1990.

Cloomly, Mrs. "Mysteries Of The Infernal Banquet; Sunday Amusements. *Weekly Visitor, Or Ladies' Miscellany.* New York: Jun 18, 1803.

"Cockney Wobble; A FEW PHRASES YOU CAN USE DOWN THE RUB. Experts Say That Rhyming Slang Will Soon Be Brown Bread, but They Must Be Having a Cow & Calf Cos It Still Seems to Be Going Ping Pong A DUB." *The People* 25 Sept. 2005.

Dabney, Lewis M. *Edmund Wilson: A Life In Literature.* Baltimore, MD: Johns Hopkins University Press, 2007.

Dalzell, Tom. *The Slang of Sin.* Springfield, MA: Merriam-Webster, 1998.

Dickson, Paul. *Words: A Collector's Compendium Of Rare And Unusual, Bold And Beautiful, Odd And Whimsical Words.* New York: Delacorte Press, 1986.

"The Doctrine of the Spontaneous Combustion of Drunkards has Just Been Exemplified in New York." *The Satirist; or, the Censor of the Time* 6 Mar. 1836.

"Drunk." *Weekly Eagle* 15 Jul. 1851.

"Drunk and Disorderly." *Punch* 20 Jul. 1872.

"Drunk and Incapable." *Moonshine* 13 Nov. 1880.

"Drunk-ology." *Bell's Life in London and Sporting Chronicle.* London, England: April 10, 1875.

Egerton, Thomas. *A Catalogue Of A General Collection Of Books, In Every Branch Of Useful And Ornamental Literature, Including Several Libraries Recently Purchased, Particularly Those Of The Late Rev. John Parkhurst...And W. Bromfield...This Day Selling...by Thomas Egerton....*London, England: 1798.

Edwards, Rob. "MacRoget's guide to Scots." *The Guardian*. 11 Aug. 1990.

"Eedjit's Guide Tae Help Yeez Chew the Fat." *The Daily Mail*. 16 Sep. 2005: 29.

Elder, Donald. *Ring Lardner: A Biography*. Garden City, NY: Doubleday, 1956.

Empey, Arthur Guy. "Over the Top." New York: G. P. Putnam's Sons, 1917.

Farmer, John Stephen and Henley, William Ernest. *Slang And Its Analogues Past And Present. A Dictionary, Historical And Comparative Of The Heterodox Speech Of All Classes Of Society For More Than Three Hundred Years*. London: Printed for subscribers only, 1890-1904.

Fergusson, Rosalind. *Shorter Slang Dictionary*. New York: Routledge, 1994.

Flexner, Stuart Berg and Soukhanov, Anne H. *Speaking Freely: A Guided Tour of American English from Plymouth Rock to Silicon Valley*. New York: Oxford, 1997. (Contains a chapter "Booze: America's Love Affair with the Bottle," which suggests dates in which terms first came into use: "inebriated" (1609), "loaded" (1886), "blotto" (1917), "smashed" (1959), and "wasted" (1984).)

Franklin, Benjamin. "The Drinker's Dictionary." *The Pennsylvania Gazette*, January 13, 1737.

Gentleman in the Navy. *The beeriad: or, progress of drink. An heroic poem, in two cantos. The first being an imitation of the first book of Mr. Pope's Dunciad; the second a description of a ram feast...By a Gentleman in the Navy. To which is annex'd a figurative moral tale*. Gosport, England: 1736.

"Getting Drunk With a Purpose." *Punch* 14 Jan. 1854.

Gloin, Lew. *The Toronto Star* 20 Apr. 1966.

Grimes, William. *Straight Up or On the Rocks—A Cultural*

History of American Drink. New York: Simon and Schuster, 1993.

Gunderson, Brian S. "Slanguage: Revisited." *Air Power History* (Summer, 2006).

Hardin, Achsah. "Volstead English." *American Speech*, 7.2 (December, 1931).

"Hints for the Almanack-Makers for 1842." *The New Satirist* 21 Nov. 1841.

Hodge, Bob, and Kam Louie. *The Politics of Chinese Language and Culture: The Art of Reading Dragons.* London: Routeledge, 1998.

Hughes, Langston. "How Many Words for Drunk?" *Daily Defender* 1 Nov. 1958.

"Intemperance." *The Boston Recorder* 17 Aug. 1822.

Johns, Bud. *The Ombibulous Mr. Mencken.* San Francisco: Synergistic Press, 1968.

Johnson, Frank. "When Is Portillo Going To Show Some Respect To Cockneys? Notebook." *Daily Telegraph* 14 Apr. 2001.

Johnson, Samuel. *A dictionary of the English language: in which the words are deduced from their originals, and illustrated in their different significations by examples from the best writers. To which are prefixed, a history of the language, and an English grammar. By Samuel Johnson, A.M. In two volumes.* London, 1755

Jorgenson, Chester E. "Benjamin Franklin and Rabelais." *The Classical Journal*, 29.7 (April, 1934).

Landers, Ann. *The Washington Post* 16 Nov. 1984.

Larson, Cedric. "The Drinkers Dictionary." *American Speech*, 12.2 (April, 1937).

Lewes, Charles Lee. *Comic Sketches, Or, The Comedian His Own Manager: Written And Selected For The Benefit Of Performers In England, Ireland, Scotland, And America.* London, England:

H.D. Symonds, 1804.

The life and adventures of Mr. Bampfylde-Moore Carew, commonly called the king of the beggars. Being an impartial account of his life...and a dictionary of the cant language, used by the mendicants. London:1779.

Lighter, J.E. "Word Improvisation: Getting Real." *The Atlantic Monthly* (February 1998): 108.

Lillo, Antonio. "Exploring Rhyming Slang in Ireland." *English World-Wide* 25.2 (1994).

London, Jack. *Martin Eden*. Review of Reviews: 1908.

Lovering, Virginia E. "Whitman Iconography; Or, Mixed Portraiture." *American Notes & Queries* 9. (1971): 134-140.

McKennon, Joe. *Circus Lingo*. Sarasota, Florida: Carnival Publishers Of Sarasota, 1980.

McKnight, George H. *English Words and Their Background*. New York: D. Appleton, 1923.

McWilliams, Brendan. "A Little Flap Over 'Three Sheets In The Wind.'" *Irish Times* 18 Apr. 2003.

Machos, Walter. "'Starched,' 'Stoned.'" *New York Times* 2 Dec. 1956.

Marnham, Patrick. *The Private Eye Story*. London: Andre Deutsch, 1982.

Mencken, H.L. *The American Language*. New York: A. A. Knopf, 1936.

Moore, Victoria. "There Are More Words to Describe the State of Inebriation Than Anything Else." *New Statesman* 17 Jun. 2002.

"Muddled and Drunk." *Funny Folks* 4 Dec. 1880.

"MULLERED." *The Mirror* 8 Dec. 2000.

Myers, James E. *A Treasury of Cocktail Humor*. Springfield, IL: The Lincoln-Herndon Press, Inc., 1994.

Nagel, Paul C. *John Quincy Adams: A Public Life, A Private*

Life. New York: Knopf, 1997.

"New Barton Vodka Aimed At Manly Men; Premium Thor's Hammer Eschewing Artful Bottle." *Crain's Business* May, 2008.

"Notes & asides." *National Review* 25 Apr. 2005 (Letters to the Editor devoted to discussion of "Three Sheets to the Wind.").

"Origin of Getting Drunk." *The Penny Satirist*. 29 Apr. 1837.

The Oxford English Dictionary. 2nd ed. 1989. OED Online. Oxford University Press: Oxford. <http://oed.com/>.

The Oxford Dictionary of English Proverbs. Oxford, England: Clarendon Press, 1935.

Pack, James. *Nelson's Blood—the Story of Naval Rum*. Annapolis, MD: Naval Institute Press, 1982.

Paine, Thomas, and other supporters of the rights of man. *Tom Paine's Jests: Being an Entirely New and Select Collection of Patriotic Bon Mots, Repartees, Anecdotes, Epigrams, Observations, etc. on Political Subjects*. London: 1794.

Palmatier, Robert A. *Food: A Dictionary of Literal and Non-literal Terms*. Westport, CT: Greenwood Press, 2000.

Parton, James. *Life and Times of Benjamin Franklin*. New York: Da Capo Press, 1971, reprint of 1864 edition.

Partridge, Eric. Paul Beale, Ed. *A Dictionary of Catch Phrases: British and American, from the Sixteenth Century to the Present Day*. London: Routledge, 1993.

Partridge, Eric. Tom Dalzell and Terry Victor, Eds. *The New Partridge Dictionary of Slang and Unconventional English*. London, England; New York : Routledge, 2006.

Pei, Mario A. *Languages for War and Peace*. New York: S.F. Vanni, 1943.

Petkovik, John. "Three Sheets To The Boiled Owl: Drinking Up The Drunktionary." *The Plain Dealer* 3 Nov. 2006.

Petry, Alice Hall. "Crane's the Bride Comes to Yellow Sky." *Explicator* 42. 1 (1983): 45-47.

Porter, Bernard H. "Some Newfoundland Phrases, Sayings, and Figures of Speech." *American Speech* (December, 1996).

"The Possibility of Getting Drunk 'Medicinally' Is Clearly Recognized by Official Authority in the Late Sentence on Lieutenant Dunbar of the Royal Marines." *The Satirist; or, the Censor of the Time* 7 Dec. 1845.

Potter Edgar R., "Frosty." *Cowboy Slang*. Phoenix, AZ: Golden West Publishers, 1985.

Potter, Humphry Tristram. *A New Dictionary Of All The Cant And Flash Languages, Both Ancient And Modern; Used By Gipsies, Beggars, Swindlers, Shoplifters By Humphry Tristram Potter Dedicated to William Addington, Esq.* The second edition. London, England: 1795.

Pound, Louise. "Franklin's 'Drinkers Dictionary' Again." *American Speech* (February, 1940).

Prenner, Manuel. "Drunk." *American Speech* 16.1 (December, 1941).

Prenner, Manuel. "Slang Synonyms for 'Drunk.'" *American Speech* 4.2 (December, 1928).

R.E.S. "The Latest Books." *Life* 16 Feb. 1922.

Rawson, Hugh. *Wicked Words*. New York: Crown Publishing, 1989.

Rollin, Lucy. *Twentieth-Century Teen Culture by the Decades: A Reference Guide*. Westport, CT: Greenwood Press, 1999.

Rooney, Andy. "From Ugly 'Sap' To Unfunny 'Drunk.'" *Chicago Tribune* 2 Apr. 1985.

Safire, William. "Drunk Again: Drunk Is A Word That Has More Jocular Slang Synonyms Than Almost Any Other, From Blotto To Pickled To Three Sheets To The Wind." *New York*

Times 31 Mar. 1985.

St. Clair, Henry. *The United States Criminal Calendar, Or, An Awful Warning To The Youth Of America: Being An Account Of The Most Horrid Murders, Pirac[i]es, Highway Robberies, &C. &C.* Boston: 1833, 1831.

Schott, Ben. *Schott's Food And Drink Miscellany.* New York: Bloomsbury, 2004.

Seal, Graham. *The Lingo: Listening to Australian English.* Sydney, NSW: University of New South Wales Press, 1999.

Seeber, Edward D. "Franklin's 'Drinkers Dictionary' Again." *American Speech* 16.1 (February, 1941).

Shay, Frank. *Drawn from the Wood: Consolations in Words & Music for Pious Friends and Drunken Companions.* New York: Gold Label Books, 1929.

Shipley, Joseph T. *Dictionary of Word Origins,* 2nd ed. New York: Philosophical Library, 1945.

Shrieves, Linda. "College Slang May Well Be Greek To You, But It's Still Way Cool." *Arizona Daily Star* 26 Aug. 2001.

Shuman, R. Baird. "Review: Words Weird and Wonderful." *American Speech* 59.3 (Autumn, 1984).

The Slang Dictionary or The Vulgar Words, Street Phrases and "Fast" Expressions of High and Low Society. Piccadilly, London: John Camden Hotten,1884.

"Slang and Sanscrit." *Punch* 4 Jun. 1859.

"Slang of the Stage." *Bismark Daily Tribune* 23 Oct. 1887.

Smith, Jack. "On Beddies, Booze, And Barf." *Los Angeles Times* 20 Aug. 1989.

Smith, Jack. "Putting Their Eggs In One Bosquet." *Los Angeles Times* 29 Sept. 1981.

"Soused Fish That Will Keep For Weeks." *The Fishing Gazette: Devoted To Angling, River, Lake & Sea Fishing And Fish Culture* 118 (1879): 358.

Spears, Richard A. *The Slang And Jargon Of Drugs And Drink.*

Metuchen, NJ: Scarecrow Press, 1986.

Spiegl, Fritz. *Keep Taking the Tabloids: What the Papers Say and How they Say It*. Pan Books: London, 1983.

"Sporting Notes." *Sporting Times* 30 Jan. 1895.

Storry, Mike, and Peter Childs. *British Cultural Identities*. London: Routledge, 2002.

Swartzlanger, Susan. "Joyce's Ulysses." *Explicator* 43.3 (1985): 29-31.

Swift, Bob. "The Military Has Always Contributed Slang To The English Language..." *The Toronto Star* 18 Feb. 1991.

Thorne, Tony. "Vamping, Chirpsing, It's A Glen: Tony Thorne Tunes In To Student Slang—Which Often Has Its Roots In The Caribbean." *The Guardian* 12 Oct. 1999.

"To Express the Condition of 45 on a Merry Pin an Honest Fellow and 46 Half Cock'd No Flincher." *New London Gazette* 13 Dec. 1771.

The Triumph Of Wit: Or, The Canting Dictionary. Being The Newest And Most Useful Academy: Illustrated With Poems, Songs, And Various Intrigues In The Canting Language, With The Explanation, &C. Dublin: 1780?

"Typography Half-Seas Over." *Punch* 3 Jun. 1854.

"Verbal Slang." *Fun* 7 Aug. 1878.

"The Vice-President of North America Drunk in the Senate." *The Derby Mercury* 22 Mar. 1865.

Wakeman, George. "Verbal Anomalies." *The Galaxy: A Magazine Of Entertaining Reading* (1866-1878): 1 Sept. 1866.

Wallrich, William J. "Barroom Slang from the Upper Rio Grande." *Western Folklore* (July, 1951).

Watson-Smyth, Kate. "Brits Have More Than A Word For It." *Austin American-Statesman* 22 Aug. 1999.

Wayfarer. "Prospectus Of A New Dictionary" (1737). *New York Observer & Chronicle* (1833-1912): 25 May 1854.

Webster, H.T. "They Don't Speak Our Language." *Forum*

and Century (December, 1933).

Webster, Noah. *A Compendious Dictionary Of The English Language: In Which Five Thousand Words Are Added To The Number Found In The Best English Compends.* Hudson & Goodwin, book-sellers, Hartford, and Increase Cooke & Co., book-sellers, New-Haven: 1806.

Webster, Noah. *An American dictionary of the English language: intended to exhibit, I. The origin, affinities and primary signification of English words, as...*Volume 1. New York: 1828. 989 pp. 2 vols.

Wentworth, Harold and Stuart Berg Flexner, compilers. *Dictionary of American Slang.* New York: Thomas Crowell, 1960.

West, Elliott. *The Saloon on the Rocky Mountain Mining Frontier.* Lincoln, NE: University of Nebraska Press, 1979. Book online.

Wilson, Edmund. *The American Earthquake—A Documentary of the Jazz Age, the Great Depression and the New Deal.* Garden City, NY: Doubleday Anchor, 1958. ("The Lexicon of Prohibition" on page 89 is Wilson's list. It is dated March 9, 1927 and lists the terms from the mildest stage to the most disastrous—"lit" to "blotto.")

Wisby, Gary. "A Slangy Guide To Drugs." *Chicago Sun-Times* 8 May 1987.

Word-Catcher. "Another Horror From The Vermin In Ermine." *The New York Times* 3 Apr. 1927.

Wright, John D. *The Language of the Civil War.* Westport, CT: Oryx Press, 2001.

Wright, Larry. *Happy as a Clam and 9,999 Other Similies.* New York: Prentice Hall General Reference, 1994.

Mike Wright's *What They Didn't Teach You about the Wild West.* Novato, CA: Presidio Press, 2000.

ACKNOWLEDGMENTS

Over the course of several decades the following friends and associates have worked to help me compile this list. They are: Jim Agenbrod, Reinhold Aman, Ryan Anthony, Russell Ash, the late poet Alan Austin, John Ballou, O.V. Barlow, John Becker, Terence Blacker, Tim Bloomfield, the late F.G. Cassidy, editor of the *Dictionary of American English*, Terry Catchpole, Philip Chaplin, the late, great slangmaster Robert L. Chapman, Mary H. Claycomb, Martha Cornog, Bill Cressey, Gina Cressey, Don Crinklaw, Kevin Cuddihy, Alan Currey, Tom Dalzell, William V. del Solar, Frank C. Dorsey, Frederick C. Dyer, Connie Eble, A. Ross Eckler of *Word Ways* and master of wordplay, Doug Evelyn, Derek Fleming, Darryl Francis, Monika Fuchs, Dan Gardner, Joseph C. Goulden, who was there at the beginning of the compilation and among the last to contribute as this book went to press, Stan Hamilton, Mim Harrison, Willliam D. Hickman, Dave Hackett, Nancy Hackett, Raymond Harris, Joyce Jackson, Jimmy Jump, Pierre Jelenc, Tony

Kalayzich, Dave Kelly, Miles Kington, W. L. Klawe, Andrew Kreig, Jack and Chris Kuppig, Rob Kyff, the word guy, Antonio Lillo, Ray Lovett, Bob Luke, Robert "Skip" McAfee, Erin McKean, John McGuire, Natalie MacLean, Peter T. Maiken, Tom Mann, Glenn Marcus, Bill Mead, Valerie Merians, Joseph C. Miller, Frederick C. Mish, Robert M. Monsen, John M. Morse, Russell Mott, Fitzhugh Mullan, Richard Nordquist, Dennis Panke, Denys Parsons, the late Charles D. Poe, Dan Rapoport, Richard E. Ray, Ross Reader, Somers Ritchie, Randy Roberts, Steve Ross, Willliam Safire, C.W. Sande, M.D., W. N. "Bill" Scott, the late David Shulman, Jon Simon, Robert Skole, Marshall L. Smith, the late Robert C. Snider, Robert Specht, Jim Srodes, Jim Steigman, William C. Stoke, Bill Tammeus, Wayne Terry, John Thornton, the late James Thorpe III, Michael Tolaydo, Elaine Viets, Stewart Wardell, Stephen Wells, the late Robert Tree West, Robb Westaley, the late Hal John Wimberley, editor of the *Goat Gap Gazette*, Mark Young for his help with the Guinness record, Philip Young and his rare collection of 19th century London slang books, and William C. Young for his work on the early manuscript.

This book is dedicated to the other compilers who have gone before me in compiling drunk lists which have made this one possible: Ambrose Bierce, Charles Dickens, J.S. Farmer, Benjamin Franklin, W.E. Henley, Langston Hughes, H. L. Mencken, Tom Paine, Eric Partridge, Richard A Spears and Edmund Wilson.

PAUL DICKSON is the author of more than 50 books. He concentrates on writing about the American language, baseball and 20th century history. He is a collector of words and wordplay whose previous lexical works include *Words*, *Names*, *Jokes*, *Toasts* and *Slang* among others. He is a consulting editor for Merriam-Webster and a contributing editor for Dover Publications and *Washingtonian* magazine. His most recent book is *Bill Veeck: Baseball's Greatest Maverick*, published in 2012.

Los Angeles-based artist and illustrator BRIAN REA is the former art director for the Op-Ed page of the *New York Times*. He enjoys bourbon on ice and has been seen along the rail at the Worthen in Lowell, MA, Chez Jay in Santa Monica, CA, and Heathers in New York City.